A fourth memento of the

Titles published by Llanteg History Society

Llanteg Down The Years (2000) – first village history and reminiscences
Llanteg: The Days Before Yesterday (2001) – second village history and reminiscences
Llanteg House Histories to 1900 (2001) - locally produced booklet
Llanteg: Turning Back The Clock (2002) – third village history and reminiscences
Grave and Memorial Inscriptions in Crunwere Parish (2002) - locally produced booklet
A Brief History of Llanteg Women's Institute 1948-2000 (2003) - locally produced booklet
Histories of Older Houses in the Parish of Crunwere 1901-2001 (2004) - locally produced booklet
Llanteg: A Century of Photographs, 1850s to 1950s (2004) – first picture book
Llanteg: A Picture Book of Memories, 1850s to 1950s (2005) – second picture book
Llanteg Village Recipe Book (2005) - locally produced booklet
Llanteg: Looking Back (2010) – fourth village history and reminiscences

Cefnogwyd gan
Supported by

ARIAN I BAWB CYMRU · AWARDS FOR ALL WALES

ARIENNIR GAN Y LOTERI
LOTTERY FUNDED

Supported by the
National Lottery
Awards for all Wales scheme

LLANTEG: LOOKING BACK

A fourth memento of the village
in words and pictures

Compiled by:

Ruth Roberts

Edited by:

Judith Lloyd

LLANTEG LOCAL HISTORY SOCIETY

Sandy-Grove, Llanteg, Narberth, Pembrokeshire, SA67 8QG, U.K.

LLANTEG: LOOKING BACK

First published in Great Britain 2010 by
LLANTEG LOCAL HISTORY SOCIETY
Sandy-Grove, Llanteg, Narberth, Pembrokeshire, SA67 8QG, U.K.

British Library Cataloguing-in-Publication Data.
A catalogue record for this book is available
from the British Library.

ISBN: 978-0-9538142-5-1

Front cover photograph - Reggie Glanville's Garage, Llanteg, 1950s

Back cover photograph - Mountain Chapel's 50th Anniversary, 1939:-
L. to R:- Mr Scourfield, Mrs Hodge, Mrs Phillips, Mrs Callen, Mrs Shanklin, Rev'd T. J. Hopkins, Mrs Williams, Miss Evans, Mrs Davies, Miss Greta Williams, Mr Ben Evans and Mr W Shanklin.
(We have no names for the two ladies sitting at the side of the chapel.)

Produced by *Manuscript ReSearch* (Book Producers)
PO Box 33, Bicester, Oxon, OX26 4ZZ, U.K. Tel: 01869 323447
Printed and bound by MWL Print Group Ltd., South Wales

PREFACE

The stories of the great and important are well recorded. However tales of the lives of ordinary folk in their small homes can easily be lost. We cannot bring these people back to life but we can record as much as possible about their existences to ensure they are never forgotten.

Well, we are here again! Amazingly, we have been able to collect still more information on Crunwere Parish to compile our fourth history book of the area. The fact that we have been able to complete four volumes still surprises us and brings our total number of publications to eleven!

It has been fascinating to see how much information there is for such a small parish – and I am sure there is still a lot left hidden in dusty corners that may never see the light of day.

You will find that throughout this and our previous books people often use the term Crunwere (Crunwear) for Llanteg (Lanteague) and vice versa. For those who do not know – Crunwere is our parish, which is roughly the area focused on by the History Society, whilst Llanteg is the village within the parish. As there is no other village within Crunwere the two names do tend to be used to mean the same thing (especially historically) – but whether properties in the very north of the parish such as Blaenhafod, Three Wells and Pantglas would say they were in 'Llanteg' is debatable.

THANKS

To begin I would like to give our heartfelt thanks to all in the community who have helped us in any way and who have put up with our questions and requests for photographs and information over the years. Everyone has been so helpful that it has not felt like work at all (well, not often)!

Whilst in no way able to name all those who have contributed to our efforts I would just like to single out a few people for individual thanks:-

Judith Lloyd for continuing to provide efficient editing and much needed advice and encouragement – even though she has now left the area and lives in Leicestershire -

Tony Brinsden and John Lewis-Tunster for their proof reading and trying to spot my mistakes -

Hugh James, who, having been born in the village in 1917, has been a vital source of local knowledge on Crunwere and its people (it is a pity that some stories were not suitable for print!!) -

Graham Mortimer for using his knowledge of the village to help us and to identify and label many old photographs -

Rose Gammon of Llanteg Garage for kindly providing us with a local outlet for our publications (and who has then had to try and answer questions about their contents) -

Manuscript Research who have now published six of our books and who have provided us with a very efficient and friendly printing service over the years -

Owen Vaughan for all the work he has put into research and also typing up the first draft of this book and contributing many articles. Owen is a member of our society despite living in Pembroke and is connected with the village through his wife's relatives (the Oriels of Garness) -

Ruth Webb, relatively a newcomer to the village and our group, who has helped me no end with the task of sorting out and tidying up the draft and offering many useful suggestions -

To the late Major David Carter of Heatherland who, as our independent referee, helped us secure funding for some of our earlier publications from the National Lottery *Awards for All Wales* scheme and who was always enthusiastic about our efforts from the very beginning -

And finally to our Community Councillor John James of Summerbrook who is our community spokesman and who has helped us secure funding for both this and our previous second Picture Book – thank you very much for your continued support of our work.

Once again we offer our thanks to all those residents of Crunwere, and many much further afield, for their support and encouragement of all our projects. We never thought when we formed our society ten years ago in March 1999 that so much of lasting worth could have come out of it – so thank you. I hope our efforts of recording information about the local people of this area will stand as a lasting monument to them all.

Most photographs included in this book are not credited as they have come from our vast collection of copies amassed over the years. So we extend a general 'thank-you' to all who have sorted out pictures for us over the years and entrusted them to our care.

We would like to apologise in advance for any errors that may be found, and we would appreciate it if these could be pointed out to us.

FOREWORD

My earliest recollection of seeing someone from another continent was when a Sikh gentleman called at our home at Oaklands in the 1950s. He was tall with a turban covering his head and a curly moustache - to a five-year-old he was pretty unusual. At first my Uncle Dan answered the door, and decided to fob the visitor off by saying "call again tomorrow". He replied in an Indian accent and with a roll of his head, "You think me come every day boss". Later in my life I met a Sikh gentleman on a flight to Karachi, and those words uttered by Uncle Dan fluttered into my mind, "You think me come every day boss", and my thoughts went back to those summer days in Llanteg when it never rained and a strange man called to sell his fine silks!

In the 1950s as a young lad I enjoyed going to the shop in Llanteg, since Peggy Bowen (The Laurels) would always give me a few boiled sweets wrapped in a brown paper bag. The shop was small and sold mainly food; it was a bit like Arkwright's shop, but without the four candles! I remember the name Wolff carved on the inside of the shop door; this was probably the work of the son of the last headmaster. Most people had a nickname in the village. One man who had tight curly hair and an eye defect was known as Colombo after the Peter Faulk character. Other names were abbreviated, like Peggy the Laurels – Cecil Oaklands – Billy the Downs – James's Broomylake – Leslie and Millie Middleton – Bevan Three Wells – Evans the Chemist. Lionel the Butcher called on Thursday and Bryn the Baker every Friday, the Co-op mobile grocery van and Bonzo called on Tuesday, also the odd travelling salesmen selling crockery and bed linen.

A man wearing a black tam, who looked French (but was more than likely not) travelled around on a bicycle selling onions. The hanks of onions hung from every available part of the bike, although my father Geoffrey said he probably had a van hidden around the corner! Whilst we lived at Oaklands our neighbour was Aunty Margaret (Rogers), and she watched over my sister and me just as if we were her real family as we grew up.

Throughout my early years at Oaklands my mother knew that if I went missing, then I could always be found with Aunty Margaret! When I look back I can't help but feel that perhaps our lives were richer then than now, for despite not having a lavish existence, we benefited greatly from friendship and good neighbours.

Roy James, Meadowcroft

CONTENTS

The Scourfield Family by George Vincent
The Wilkin Family of Amroth and Crunwere by Owen J.Vaughan
20th Century Crunwere
Some Notes on Mountain Chapel by Ruth Roberts
Mountain Chapel – Cambria Archaeology Survey – 2002/3 by Ruth
Roberts
1904 Sales Notice (Crunwere Farm and Rigmanhill) by Ruth Roberts
Llanteglos House Sale 1903 and 1940 by Ruth Roberts
The South Pembrokeshire Dialect in the Llanteg Locality by Noel
H.Davies
Extracts from Crunwere-related Newspaper Articles by Ruth Roberts
Extracts from St Elidyr's Church Minute Book 1941-80 by Ruth Roberts
Early 20th Century Obituaries by Ruth Roberts
    Charles Allen 1939
    Mary Davies 1928
    Evelyn Ebsworth 1931
    W.J.Ebsworth 1937
    James Price John 1937
    Elizabeth Raymond 1939
    Sarah Reynolds 1933
    Mary Jane Willment 1944
    Elizabeth Wolff 1937
Reminiscences
Margaret Carter (née Hawes)
Alun Davies – Memories of Milton Farm
Elvie Davies – Memories of Crunwere
Kathleen Davies (née Morse)
Ruth Davies (née Williams)
Maureen Ebsworth (née Ebsworth)
Jean Gardner (née Howells)
Kenneth George
Alwyn James
Audrey James (née Rowlands)
Betty James (née Shepherd)
Hugh James
Ray James (née Davies)
Roy James
Kay Scourfield (née Scourfield)
Avrenah Tremlett (née Jones)
George Vincent

Christmas Customs
Betty Bevan
Margaret Brinsden
Margaret Carter
Noel Davies
Elizabeth Dee
Noel Ebsworth
Delmi Evans
Jean Gardner
Doreen Glanville
Lyn Harcombe
Josephine Jenkins
Nancy John
Violet Merriman
Beryl Payne
Kathleen Phillips
James Smart
Laura Thomas
Peter Thomas
George Vincent
Appendix
Llanteg History Society Members by Ruth Roberts
Bibliography

MAP OF VILLAGE

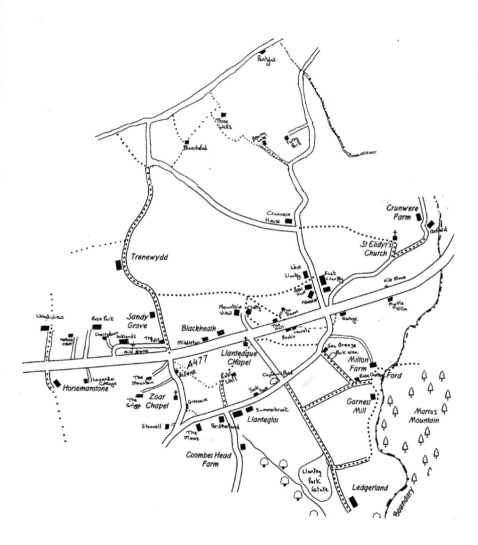

CRUNWERE IN THE EARLY YEARS
POPULATION FIGURES (1536-1815)
by Ruth Roberts

Crunwear –

1563	**1670**	**1801**
(No. of households)	(No. of Hearth Tax payers)	(No. of families)
25	34	44

Pembrokeshire County History Volume VIII
Narberth Hundred, Page 6

CRUNWERE WILLS PROVED AT THE ECUMENICAL
CHURCH COUNCIL OF ST DAVIDS 1600 - 1857
by Owen J.Vaughan

1609 Mathewe White, of Crunwere
   (buried at Crunwere near father's grave. Among
   other debtors mentioned are George Dawkyne,
   Rector of Crunwere and David the Smith of
   Llanteg)

1611 William Hibart, Carpenter of Crunwere

1620 Edward Will, Yeoman of Crunwere

1623 Robert Elliott, buried at Crunwere

1684 Samuell Edmund, Yeoman of Crunwere

1684 Reignald Howell, Trenewydd, Crunwere
   (among others mentioned are his brother, John
   Howells, Rector of Llanfyrnach and his eldest son,
   also John Howells, Rector of New Radnor)

1738 Dorothy Davies, Widow of Crunwere
   (also mentions among others William Thomas,
   Carpenter of Crunwere and her brother Philip
   Saunders, Gent of Pendine)

1771 John Philip, Mason of Crunwere
   (also mentioned was his daughter Jane, wife of
   Evan Lewis, Mason of Crunwere)

1775 Elizabeth Harries, Widow of Crunwere

1788 Mary Oriel, Spinster of Crunwere
   (youngest daughter of the late Thomas Oriel,
   Carpenter & Miller of Garness, Crunwere. Also

mentions her brother William Oriel,
Churchwarden of Llanddowror and Forester to Sir
R.B.Phillips)

1792   Thomas Williams, Miller of Crunwere
(mentioned was daughter Sarah Williams and her
two guardians: Richard Williams and William
Oriel - brother to Sarah's mother Elizabeth)

1800   Thomas Oriel, Carpenter of Garness
(died 1782, estate caused court case involving
Mary Oriel 1788 and Thomas Williams 1792 plus
others)

1803   David Wilkin, Bowmans Pit, Crunwere

1805   Francis Thomas, Rigmans Hill, Crunwere
(mentioned was the freehold of Rigman Hill and
Brinny Lake)

1814   William Davies, Yeoman of Crunwere

1814   Elizabeth Howells, Llanteague, Crunwere
(among others mentioned was George son of
Thomas Mends by her niece Elizabeth Gwynne,
widow)

1822   Henry John, Yeoman of Long Parks, Crunwere

1830   Richard Llewelling, farmer of Llanteague

1839   Thomas Dalton, Rector of Crunwere
(mentions his son James, Gent of 'Norton or Lower
Lantegue', Crunwere)
(Research note: Clearly this is not the Thomas
Dalton, Clergyman, mentioned in the 1841 census
from Rhos Crowther. See Research Notes on 'The
Dalton Family' later in this draft)

1843   William Waters, Farmer of Crunwere Bush, Crunwere
(valued at under £20. Also mentions Richard
Morgan, Vicar of Kiffig, the son of Robert Morgan,
Gent of Trenewydd)

1849   James Price, Ledgerland, Crunwere

1851   Ann McIntyre, Spinster of Crunwere
(valued at under £200)

1857   William Thomas, Farmer of Griggs, Crunwere
(mentions New Chapel on Griggs Farm and the
Baptist Chapel Trustees).

THE INVENTORY OF REIGNALD HOWELL OF TRENEWYDD – 1686

transcribed and set out in this format by Owen J.Vaughan

A true and perfect inventory of all ye goods cattels and avourit of Reignald Howell of ye parish of Crunwere in the Archdeacon Diocese of St David's Gent lately deceased taken and apprised ye 22nd day of June anno Rgi Rgs James 2nd nane Anglise & secundo by ye persons subscribed.

In the Hall
Three small table board and joyned stooles one old
settler and forms and chairs and 3 carpets 5
cussions one hal brush valued at   02 00 06

In ye Dinning Room
One Bed furnished, one table board, one livery Cupboard
2 chairs and 10 joyn'd stools 8 cussions 4 window curtains
2 carpetts one cupboard Cloath Two old boxes and two
remnant of Cloath at   08 00 00

In the Red Chamber
One standing bed furnished 1 Truckler bed 1 table
board 1 Cupboard 7 chairs one stolle one trunk 1 looking
glass 1 old clock 2 window curtains 2 carpetts
one table cloath one cloe stoole   08 18 06

In the Kitching Chamber
One standing bed & Truckler bed furnished 3 old
chests 3 small boxes one trunk one chair one Close stoole   04 00 00

In ye Further Chamber
One bed furnished 3 stools 3 old chairs one box 2 window
curtains one looking glass   02 05 00

In ye Little Chamber
One bed furnished 2 chests 3 boxes one trunk   01 00 00

In the Cock loft over the Kitchen
One old bed for servants with other lumber   00 05 00

In the Cock Loft over ye Dining Room
3 old Bedsteeds one old cupboard and chest a small parcel
of wool an parcel of maul (?) (*unreadable*) a parcel of feathers
with other lumber   03 00 00

In the Dayry
A parcel of wooden and earthen vessell one cheese press
with other lumber   00 06 08

In the Kitching
One old Jack a pair of (h) and Irons with spits pewter
brass a Birding (?) (*unreadable*) trenches and other wooden
vessills   07 13 04
In the Cellar
A parcel of Bottles glasses earthen ware and wooden
vessills   00 06 08
Corn in the house and haggard valued at   06 06 08
One Hive of Bees at   00 02 06
Carts, ploughs and other implements of husbandry
with some timbre and other lumber   08 00 00
Corn in ye ground valued at   20 17 04
Plate valued at   07 04 00
Linnen of all sorts and a small remnant of ffannell   04 06 08
Thirteen cowes and a bull valued at   21 00 00
Eight oxen valued at   16 00 00
Ten young cattle of 3 year old at   10 03 04
Six young cattle of 2 years old at   04 00 00
Ffive yearlings at   01 13 04
Eight calves at   01 12 00
Nine horses and mares and one colt at   13 06 08
Fforty five sheep at   06 15 00
Thirty 3 lambs at   03 06 00
Piggs and Poultry at   03 06 08
Debts due to ye Testator and moneys in ye house   25 18 06
Books wearing apparell house and furniture valued at 12 00 00

John Howell
Thomas Reignald
Rob Ferrior

(2 *words unknown*) Reignald Howell of Trenewydd in the parish of
Cronweare in the County of Pembroke.
Elizabeth Howell and John Howell Executors, June 28 Ano Dmi 1686
Geo Owen (Ref:SD/1689)

AMROTH INSCRIPTIONS
by Owen J.Vaughan
'Near this wall lie the bodies of John Wolfe late of Merrixton son of

Roger Woolf Gent and first husband of Rebecca sister of John Poyer of (*word unreadable*) Gent, who died Jan 27 – 1720 aged 27.

And of her second husband William Davies youngest son of Chancey Davies late of **Lanteague**, Gent who died April 30 1725 aged 28.'

'Sacred to the memory of Henry Child who departed this life December the 16th 1805 aged 85 years.

Also Alice Child *(née Oriel)* his wife is buried here in same grave. She departed this life November 27th 1816 aged 91 years.

This stone was erected by Thomas Child in affectionate remembrance of his parents.'

JURY SERVICE AVAILABILITY IN CRUNWERE 1786 – 1900
by Owen J.Vaughan

Since the act of 1692 strict criteria had been laid down as to who in each parish would be available to perform Jury service. In the listing for Little Newcastle of 16 September 1808, the constable, Henry Lewis Petty, gives us a full and clear picture of these qualifications which also holds good for the Parish of Crunwere and thus gives us some indication of the monetary value of village members during this period.

Quote: A true list containing the Name and Places of Abode together with the title and additions of all persons between the ages of 21 and 70 (years) dwelling within the Parish of Little Newcastle qualified to serve on juries, that is to say of every person that has in his own name or in trust for him within the County aforesaid six pounds a year above – Reprizes of freehold or Copyhold land and tenements or of lands and tenements and ancient demerece or in rents or in all or any of their in fee simple feetail or for the life of himself or some other person on having land in procession in his own right of £20 a year above the reserved rent being hold by lease of five hundred years or more or for 99 years or any other term and determinable on one or more lives.

Records are missing for 1836 – 1876 inclusive except for 1846 which has a list for Tenby St Mary out Liberty only.

Assuming that members of the parish remained in the same abode for the years that the returns for Jury service are missing, then for the periods 1786 – 1835 and 1877 – 1900, we are able to produce the following table for Crunwere:-

NAME	PERIOD Fm 1825	TITLE	OCCUP	ABODE
David Ormond	1790 – 1800			Trenewydd
William Davis	1790 – 1800			Crunwere Beech
Francis Thomas	1790 – 1796			Rigmans Hill
Thomas Griffith	1795 – 1796			Mountain
William Beynon	1800 only			
Richard Llewhelling	1796 – 1823		Farmer	Lanteague
John Henry Martin	1805 only		Squire	
William Reymond	1796 – 1815			Lanteague
Will(iam) Thomas	1805 – 1823			Greigs
Thomas Highway	1809 – 1811			Trenewydd
James Martin Esq.	1802 only			Trenewydd
Robert Morgan(s)	1815 – 1835	Lease/Cpy hld	Farmer	Trenewydd
Benjamin Morris	1816 – 1835	Leasehold	Farmer	Lanteague
James Price	1816 – 1835	Leasehold	Farmer	Ledgerland
James Dalton	1820 – 1823			Norton
Thomas Oriel	1820/1825/ 1832-35	Freehold	Farmer	Garnass
David Reymond	1821 – 1835	Leasehold	Farmer	Crunwere
Edward Page	1825 – 1826	Leasehold	Farmer	Three Wells
Thomas William	1825 – 1828	Leasehold	Farmer	Griegs
Thomas Oriel	1826 only	Freehold	Millard	Garnass Mill
John Hancock	1878	Occupier	Farmer	Crunwere
John William	1878-1883	Occupier	Farmer	Lanteague
William James	1878	Occupier	Miller	Garnass Mill
David Jones	1878-1883	Occupier	Farmer	Three Wells
Richard Morris	1878-1881	Occupier	Farmer	Lanteague
Lloyd R.Phillips	1878 only	Occupier	Farmer	Oaklands
David Williams	1878-1883/ 1887-1900	Occupier	Farmer	Trenewydd
Peter Downs	1881-1883	Freeholder	Doctor MD	Lanteague House
John Hancock	1881 only	Occupier	Farmer	Crunwere Farm
David Morris	1881-1883	Occupier	Farmer	Furzy Park
Evan James	1883/1887	Freeholder	Farmer	Summerbrook
Stephen Lewis	1883 only	Freeholder	Farmer	Blaenhavod
John James	1885-1899	Occupier	Farmer	Garnass Mill
William John	1887 only	Occupier	Farmer	Unidentified
James S.Morris	1887-1891	Occupier	Farmer	Furzy Park
James S.Morris	1892-1900	Occupier	Farmer	Three Wells
Walter Williams	1891 only	Occupier	Farmer	Rigman Hill

NAME	PERIOD Fm 1825	TITLE	OCCUP	ABODE
William W.Williams	1892-1897	Freeholder	Traveller (?)	Milton
Benjamin H.Morris	1894-1900	Occupier	Farmer	Furzy Park
Benjamin Jones	1895-1900	Freeholder	Farmer	Heatherland
John Edwards	1898-1900	Occupier	Farmer	Milton
William W.Williams	1898-1900	Freeholder	Farmer	Lawrells
James C.S.Glanville	1897-1900	Freeholder	Farmer	Lanteague

GENERAL ELECTIONS (1812 AND 1831) – BUT NOT AS WE KNOW THEM
by Owen J.Vaughan

From the 16th to the 21st October of 1812 and 10th to 26th May of 1831 voting took place to elect the Pembrokeshire Member of Parliament. In 1812 those standing were John Owen Esq. and (*unknown*) Campbell and in 1831 Sir John Owen of Orielton and the Hon. Robert Fulke Greville. Voting took place over 5 days in 1812 and over 16 days in May of 1831, with a written record by Hundred being kept of who voted and for whom. From this Pembrokeshire Parliamentary Election Poll Book it is possible to compile the following table for the Parish of Crunwere, to show who voted and where their parliamentary loyalties lay.

In 1812 the voting was as follows:-

Electors Name	Place of Abode	Qualification	Place voted for Parish	Parish	Voted for
Rev'd John Jenkins	Mydrim	Freehold	Lanteague	Crunwere	Campbell
Griffith Howell	Llanteague	Leasehold at Lanteague	Lanteague	Crunwere	Campbell
Richard Llewhellin	Llanteague	Leasehold	Lanteague	Crunwere	Campbell
George Child	Crunwere	Leasehold	Pearlinghill	Crunwere	Campbell
John Lewes	Crunwere	Leasehold	Downs	Crunwere	Campbell
William Thomas	Crunwere	Freeholder	Griggs	Crunwere	Owen
Rev'd Thomas Dalton	Crunwere Parish	Freehold	Tithe & Glebe Lands	Crunwere	Campbell
William Davies	Crunwere	Freehold	Brimmylake	Crunwere	Owen
Theops John	Crunwere Parish	Leasehold	Clynne Bush	Crunwere	Campbell
James Oriel	Crunwere Parish	Freehold	Garnass Rock	Crunwere	Campbell
Thomas Roblin	Crunwere Parish	Leasehold	Lanteague	Crunwere	Owen
John William Hughes	Carms Tregile	Freeholder	Mountain	Crunwere	Owen
Thomas Oriel	Crunwere	Leaseholder	Garnass Mill	Crunwere	Campbell

Research notes: a. Clynne Bush probably is Crunwere Bush.

           b From previous research, Garnass Rock is known to be Garnass Farm.

           c Pearlinghill probably is Perlin Hill.

In May of 1831 the voting was as follows:-

Electors Name	Place of Abode	Qualification	Place voted for Parish	Parish	Occupier	Voted for
Thomas Oriel	Garnass Mill	Freehold	Garnass	Crunwere	Himself	Greville
Thomas Dalton, Clerk	Crunwere the Church and Tythes	Beneficie the Church and Tythes	Beneficie	Crunwere	Himself	Greville
James Dalton	Lanteague	Leaseholder	Lanteague	Crunwere	Himself	Greville
William Thomas	Griggs	Freeholder	Griggs	Crunwere	Himself	Greville
Benjamin Morris	Lanteague	Leaseholder	Leanteague	Crunwere	Himself	Greville
William Morris	Stepaside	Leaseholder	Milton	Crunwere	John James	Greville
James Lewis	Downs	Leaseholder	Downs	Crunwere	Himself	Greville
George Child	Perlins Hill	Leaseholder	Perlins Hill	Crunwere	Himself	Greville
William Raymond	Lanteague	Rent Charge	Rent Charge out of Lanteague	Crunwere	Benjamin Morris	Greville
John Jenkins, Clerk	Midrim	Freeholder	Lanteague	Crunwere	John Jenkins	Owen
Theophilus John	Clynne Bush	Leaseholder	Clynne Bush	Crunwere	Himself	Greville
Griffith Wilkin	Clynne Bush	Leaseholder	Clynne Bush	Crunwere	Himself	Greville
David Lewis	Crunwere	Leaseholder	Part of Trenewydd	Crunwere	Himself	Greville
William Lewis	Trenewydd	Leaseholder	Part of Trenewydd	Crunwere	Himself	Greville
James David	Broomy-lake	Leaseholder	Broomylake	Crunwere	Himself	Owen
David Harry	Lanteague	Leaseholder	Part of Lanteague	Crunwere	Himself	Owen
Benjamin Thomas	Trenewydd	Leaseholder	Part of Trenewydd	Crunwere	Himself	Owen
John James	Milton	Leaseholder	Milton	Crunwere	Himself	Owen
David Raymond	Crunwere	Leaseholder	Crunwere	Crunwere	Himself	Greville

This is not the place to describe the highly charged and acrimonious debates and exchange of insults that took place at these elections and indeed are much better described elsewhere. Suffice to say, disappointment must have been great within the village, with Sir John Owen winning both elections. Owen's win in the

May 1831 election was short lived when he was again opposed by Greville in October of that year. However, on the ninth day of voting, in pouring rain, Greville again conceded defeat. Both campaigns had been ruinous to the contestants, mainly, it would appear, due to the rather none too subtle ways they tried to entice the voters. It has been noted that Greville had innkeepers' bills exceeding £15,000 in 1831; one wonders just how much of that was owed to the hostelries of The Golden Lion and Royal Oak in Crunwere (I hope a goodly amount).

Parliamentary Poll Book - Pembs Record Office Ref: PQ/RP/P/1 & 6.

CRUNWERE MILESTONES
by Ruth Roberts

Our parish can boast two milestones, one at either end of Llanteg. These milestones show the distance to Hobb's Point in the west and Carmarthen in the east (with the Oaklands one showing 18 miles to Carmarthen and 15 miles to Hobb's Point) and are marked at their foot by the manufacturer – Moss & Sons 1838.

With the help of Carmarthen Library mention has been found in trade directories of a William Moss and Son, iron founders in Blue Street, Carmarthen (1835). William Moss also had Ironmongers, Plumbers, Braziers and Tinplate Works at Guildhall Square, Carmarthen. Earlier in the 19th century William Moss of Carmarthen also issued copper trade tokens which read:-

PAYABLE BY WILLM MOSS CARMARTHEN – SWANSEA –
AND AT JACOB & HALSE LONDON 1813
(shown within a wreath of oak and acorns).

(Trade tokens appeared when the supply of regal coins was inadequate.) These tokens were manufactured by Halliday of Birmingham.

Photo: Ruth Roberts

County Boundary Stone between Carmarthenshire and Pembrokeshire, set into Castle Ely Bridge - the stream which runs underneath is the boundary. This bridge, once the main route into Pembrokeshire, is now on a quiet loop of road since the A477 was straightened in the 1980s.

We also have a County boundary stone set into Castle Ely Bridge as the stream beneath is the actual County and Parish border – there are no maker's marks on this item.

THE POOR OF CRUNWERE PARISH
by Ruth Roberts

The Guardian for Amroth district was Mr Thomas Purser of Craig-y-Borion, later to move to Llanteglos. The Crunwere Guardians were Rev'd W.D.Phillips, followed by Mr David Williams, Trenewydd, with the Assistant Overseer being Mr John Davies, Greenacre (who was paid £10 per year).

In the six months up to 25 March 1881 there were eleven families living in Crunwere Parish who were receiving out-relief from the Narberth Union:-

Name	Age	Residence	Amount (Week)	Cause
Mary Griffiths	77	Lanteague	2s	Old Age
Margaret Rogers	65	Lanteague	1s & 6d	Debility
John James and Wife	72 & 74	Milton Back	2s & 6d	Age
Sophia Raymond	76	Commons	2s & 6d	Age
Mary Thomas	69	Cyffig	4s	Debility
Ann Evans	80	Lanwinio	2s & 6d	Age
Griffith Wilkins	87	Bush	Various	Age
Jane Edwards	45	Lanteague	2s	Debility
John Lewis	76	Lanteague	1s 6d	Age
W.Griffiths and Wife	84 & 84	Lanteague	8s	Age & ?
Elizabeth Lewis	69	Revel Wall	2s	Age

(Researcher O.J.Vaughan note: John James and Wife equate to John and Ada James whose son John James was currently farming at Garnass Mill Farm, whilst next door at Garnass Rock also known as Garnass Farm, their daughter Sarah was the wife of farmer John Oriel.)

Some other individuals mentioned during the period 1872–1882 receiving out-relief at home were:-

Year	Name	Residence	Age	Cause
1872	Sarah Thomas	Folly	Unknown	Age
1873	D.Evans & Wife	Zoar	80 & 71 years	Age

23

Year	Name	Residence	Age	Cause
1875	Wm Oriel & Wife	Lanteague	50 & 48 years	Wife's Illness
1875	Martha Palmer	Crunwere	69 years	Age
1876	Elizabeth Reynolds	Milton	37 years	Widow with 8 Children
1876	Ann Evans	Zoar	76 years	Age
1876	Jane Evans	Bevlin	80 years	Age
1877	Jane Edwards	Lanteague	49 years	Ill-Health
1877	Martha Palmer	Lanteague	71 years	Old Age **
1880	T. Mends	Common	78 years	Idiot
1880	Dan Thomas	Lanteague	Not shown	Temporary

(** = Later to be found in Carmarthen Asylum)

In 1878 Jane Raymond (aged 8 years) of Lanteague was shown as an orphan. In 1879 she was shown as of Crunwear and the cause of the out-relief was 'schooling'.

Individuals were also shown who were admitted to St David's Asylum, Carmarthen. It is not known whether the three 'Thomas' inmates were related:

1872	Caroline Thomas from Crunwere.
1873	Caroline Thomas and Robert Thomas from Crunwere.
1875	Caroline Thomas, Robert Thomas and Sarah Thomas from Crunwere.
1876	Caroline Thomas and Robert Thomas from Crunwere.
1877	Martha Palmer from Crunwere, in addition to the above Caroline and Robert Thomas.

The venue for compulsory vaccinations for the Amroth and Crunwere area was at the Commercial Inn (near Kilanow crossroads, later called The Stagecoach, and now a private house). The vaccinations were given on the 2nd, 3rd and 4th Fridays of April and October at 2pm.

With information from *Narberth Union Abstract and History of Paupers 1872 – 1882.*

EARLY LLANTEG INQUESTS
by Ruth Roberts

Peter Phelps of Trelessy Farm, 60 years old, farmer – died 22 October 1887.
Inquest held on 24th at Trelessy.
Verdict –'Accidentally fell over a cliff'.
James Merrilees of Stanwell Villa, 80 years old, retired farmer – died

14 March 1896.

Inquest held on 16th at Greenacre.

Verdict – 'Died from natural causes'.

William James of Broomylake, 77 years old, farmer – died 15 September 1897.

Inquest held on 18th at Broomylake.

Verdict – 'Died from injuries – the result of accidentally falling from the roof of a house on which he was working'.

John Jenkins of Lanteague, 55 years old, mason – died 3 January 1900.

Inquest held on 5th at Lanteague Farm.

Verdict – 'Was found drowned but how drowned there is not sufficient evidence to show'.

William Davies, Oaklands – died 22 May 1902.

Verdict – 'Death by accident'.

Mary Ann Hughes, Oxford – died 23 July 1904.

Verdict – 'Death by natural causes'.

Register of Inquests Held - Pembrokeshire Record Office.

OLD LLANTEG FAMILIES

The first eight articles all have ancestors and connections with the Davies family which originated from the marriage between John David (later changed to Davies) and Elizabeth Bevan in 1793 – both supposedly from Ludchurch. However the following has now come to light but we have not yet had time to follow it up.

Deed of gift of messuages and land called Brimmey Lake (*Broomylake*) and Rhydgoch in Crunwear, in exchange for food and lodging.

Parties: -

1. John Davies of Crunwear, Gent
2. William Davies of Crunwear, tailor, John's reputed son, and Jane his wife.

(Researcher O.J.Vaughan note: It appears that Lewis and James acted as Solicitors for the Davies family over many years, and then possibly acted as solicitors for parties occupying premises previously owned by the Davies family in Crunwere.)

D/LJ/2072 9th May 1769 number 12.

The Allens of Crunwear
by Howard G.Allen

The story of Old William Allen of Crunwear is enough to test the patience of any family historian. The 1901 census shows him, at the age of 75, living with his second wife, Elizabeth (Thomas), aged 76, at Rose Cottage. The puzzle centres on the 'grandson', George A.Wilmington, aged 15, who is with them. Old William had a sister, Elizabeth Allen, who married a Henry Wilmington and gave birth to a son. It seems that Elizabeth was taken ill and Old William's daughter Jane was sent to look after her. When Elizabeth died, Henry married Jane Allen and they had a large family, one of whom was George A.Wilmington, the same one who appears as Old William's grandson in 1901.

Thus Henry Wilmington was the boy's father and his great-uncle! The Wilmingtons seem to have had connections with Kent and young George married a lady from there in 1909.

Perhaps I should mention that Jane was Old William's daughter by his first wife, Frances Smith.

The only other Allen in the 1901 census for Crunwear was John, a blacksmith aged 38, who was living at Milton Back with his wife 'Jennette' Elisabeth (née Davies), aged 26, and their two very young children, William Thomas Allen and Charles Smith Allen.

John and Jennette Elizabeth Allen, Rose Cottage

Willie Allen,
Rose Cottage
(son of
John & Jennette Elizabeth) -
later to become
the village postman

Old William and John were descendants of Stephen Allen (c1749-1787) and Rachel Powell, of whom little is known except that they were married in 1773 at St. Elidyr. Most (but not all) of the Allens in the coal-mining parishes of South Pembrokeshire are descended from them and many were either coal miners or blacksmiths. Indeed I trace my own ancestry to Stephen and Rachel through the Allens of Sardis.

It is a curious fact that before the railways encouraged the dispersal of workers around the country, the only Allens in Wales were to be found in South Pembrokeshire (except for a few outliers in the Gower). Were they all related, where did they come from, and how did they get there?

Much of the information above is based on research originally carried out by Bill Allen (USA) and Dennis Allen (deceased, formerly of Northumberland). Details of the Australian connection, especially the Wilmingtons, are mainly from Phil O'Brien (Australia). Using this material and my own studies of gravestones, census records etc. I have assembled fairly comprehensive details about the descendants of Stephen and Rachel, about which I can be contacted through Llanteg History Society.

27

Ancestors of Alfred James (1859-1950)
by Ruth Roberts

In our previous history books you may have read of how Alfred James built many properties in and around Llanteg. Alfred was the grandfather of Hugh James, Arfryn, Llanteg, who, like his father Howard and grandfather Alfred, was also a builder.

*Bertie James, ?,
father Alfred James
and wife Mary*

The 1901 census shows Alfred as 41 years old and classed as a stonemason, living at Broomylake, Llanteg, with his wife Elizabeth (36 years and born in Amroth parish) and their four children – Howard, Evelyn, Herbert and William. Also living there were his brother and sister-in-law, Jane and Thomas Phillips (stonemason), both born in Amroth. Alfred and Elizabeth had been married at Crunwere Church in June 1888, both being able to sign their names. Elizabeth was a servant at Lanteague (probably now East Llanteg) and her father was John Phillips (shoemaker).

On the 1861 census Alfred is shown as a little boy of 1 year, living at what was called Broomy Lodge, the son of William and Jane James. William was classed as a mason and while Jane's place of birth was shown as Crunwere, William shows his variously as Crunwere and Laugharne.

From the 1851 census it appears that Jane may have been born Jane Davies, as William's sister-in-law, Mary Davies, was living with them at

Broomy Lake. Jane Davies may have been the young 20 year old girl Jane David (*sic*), shown as a servant at Trenewydd, Llanteg, in 1841. Her family could have been Jane and James Davies who were living at Broomy Lake in 1841.

In 1841 William James (Alfred's father) was shown as a mason at Toads Grove, Llanteg, son of Thomas and Jane James (53 and 50 yrs). William, 21 yrs, is shown as being born in the county so perhaps he was correct when he shows his birthplace as Amroth (but possibly putting Laugharne as his place of birth as his mother was from Llansadurnen and he could have been born there). In 1851 Thomas and Jane James were shown living at Frogs Valley (possibly The Valley of today) with Thomas being 57 years (a labourer of 10 acres) and born at Llangwm and Jennet (*sic*) 59 years and born at Llansadurnen – their grandson William (5 yrs) was living with them.

Alfred would sometimes live close to where he was working – staying in Lampeter Velfrey whilst building Brynsion School. Alfred lived at Mountain View when working on Amroth Vicarage (now Hanover Court) which was why he was unable to be involved with the building of Mountain Chapel which occurred at the same time.

Alfred was therefore one of a long line of builders/stonemasons, beginning with William James and stretching down through five generations to reach Ross James today (Hugh's son).

My Mason/Lewis/James Ancestors
Six Generations of a Family in Llanteg
by David Mason

In the winter of 1906/7 two young children arrived in the village of Crunwear. Three-year-old Herbert Mason and his baby sister Annie must have attracted many a sympathetic glance as they settled in at their grandparents' home, for in a small, tight-knit community everyone would have heard of the tragedy that had struck the family.

Elizabeth Ann Mason, the children's mother, was well-known in Crunwear, and must have had a reputation as a capable woman who had seen something of the world. She had grown up in the village, the eldest daughter of John and Sarah James, and would have helped look after her nine younger brothers and sisters and her widowed grandmother, Eliza Lewis, who shared their home at Ruelwall.

We can guess that Elizabeth would have been expected to leave the crowded family home and stand on her own two feet as soon as possible. At the age of 13, in 1891, she was working as a servant for farmer John

Davies at Ivy Cottage. Ten years later she had found her way to Neath as a parlour maid in the home of solicitor Arthur Williams. Many villagers would not have travelled so far in their lives or come into such close contact with the upper classes.

Elizabeth married Alfred Mason, a labourer from St Issells in 1902 and Herbert was born the next year. Annie followed in 1906, but just months after her birth, at the age of 28, Elizabeth's life was cut short by an epileptic fit. Family lore has it that it was Herbert who found his mother, drowned in a puddle in the garden of their home at Churchton.

Alfred now faced the awful prospect of losing not only his wife but his children. How could he care for them and still earn a living? Dr Barnardos was a real possibility, Annie later recalled, until Sarah and John stepped in. The children must have spent more than a year with them at Ruelwall until Alfred remarried and they were able to return to his home.

Herbert Mason, my grandfather, grew up to become the blacksmith at New Hedges, but he maintained his connections with Llanteg all his life. He seems to have been particularly close to Rett, Elizabeth's eldest sister, who may have become something of a second mother to him during that traumatic period at Ruelwall. My father, Haydn, remembers childhood trips to Sparrowsnest to see Auntie Rett and Uncle Jim Davies.

Annie became a lady's companion and worked in Bristol for the Wills family, who helped found Imperial Tobacco and Bristol University. She married George Richards, who farmed at Trevaughan Farm, Whitland, and she died there in 2004, surviving her brother by 30 years.

✶✶✶✶✶✶✶✶✶✶✶✶✶✶

The family ties with Llanteg go back generations with connections on both sides. Elizabeth Ann's great-great-grandfather, Henry John, was born in 1750. Henry married Sarah Llewellin at St Elidyr's Amroth, in 1780, and they are buried in its churchyard.

Henry, a yeoman farmer, leased a property called Longparks, near where Zoar Baptist Chapel was later built. He died aged 72 leaving two shillings and sixpence to each of his seven children at his death from an estate worth less than £10. Touchingly, he also bequeathed to his unmarried daughters the right to use his best room 'with a good bed and also a fire to sit by, when sick or sore and cannot follow their daily Labour'.

Henry's daughter Mary married William Lewis, the son of David and Jinnet Lewis, of Amroth. In 1841 he was farming 52 acres and they lived at Crygyborrion farmhouse to the west of the village. However they spent most of their lives at The Barrietts (*now Caldey View*) and Mary – 'Mollie the Barrietts' - was known for her herbal remedies at a time when the nearest doctor or chemist was in Narberth. (She is mentioned in one of many articles by Ben Price about his memories of local life, referred to in *Llanteg Down the Years* p. 45.)

William's eldest son Henry married Eliza Rees, a collier's daughter from Amroth, who had been working as a servant for his neighbours at Crygyborrion. Her father, William, may be the same William Rees who was recorded as one of 49 inmates at the Narberth Workhouse in 1841 and lived there until his death five years later. If so, he would have witnessed the events in 1843 when several hundred Rebecca Rioters attacked the building and had to be dispersed by the Castlemartin Yeomanry.

Henry and Eliza lived most of their married life at Milton Cottage, bringing up six children. Henry worked as a labourer. Ben Price recalls Harry Lewis of Milton and Robert Evans of Honeypot Hill being in charge of one of two lime kilns at Trenewydd Farm (*Llanteg Down the Years* p. 41). Eliza survived Henry by 15 years, and, after his death in 1874, she left their final home at Mountain and went to live with their daughter Sarah and her husband John James at Ruelwall. Henry and Eliza are buried together at St Elidyr's, Crunwear.

****

Robert Evans's father David, born in Crunwear around 1795-8, was Alfred Mason's great grandfather, and had also worked as a lime burner. He lived at Trelifey (or Trelissey), south of the village, with his wife Margaret (born Margaret John) and their five daughters. He seems to have done well for himself and by 1848 he had started farming.

David was a prominent member and deacon of the local Baptist community and was closely involved in the construction of Zoar Chapel in 1854, doing most if not all of the haulage for free. The chapel was built at a cost of £60 with a further £20 spent on a two-room lean-to cottage at the side to be used as a caretaker's house. It was built on part of the field called Long Park, the property which 40 years earlier had been leased by Henry John. The building is now a Chapel of Rest and the caretaker's home is the mortuary (*Llanteg Down the Years* pp 24 and 28).

Margaret died in 1850 and David seems to have remarried. The 1861 census lists a David Evans from Crunwear, aged 64, who was living over the river in Cabin, Marros, with his wife, Anne, and her two sons. His son, Robert, was living in the next house, Honeypot Hill. However, this episode is something of a mystery. I can find no marriage certificate and no sign of David or his new family in the 1871 census.

David died of old age at Zoar, the caretaker's cottage at the Baptist Chapel, and his gravestone is in Zoar yard. He was 78 and his profession was given as farm labourer. Margaret is buried at Amroth Church, where her broken gravestone can be seen leaning against the wall. Perhaps she would have been buried at Zoar if the chapel had existed when she died, or maybe David's Baptist faith came to mean much more to him in the 23 years after her death.

David's daughter Elizabeth married Joseph Mason, the son of James Mason, a labourer from Gumfreston in 1848. They were both working as servants at the time, but Joseph turned to labouring after their marriage. They moved to Stackpole Elidor but returned to the village briefly and Maria Mason, the third of their six children, was born at Bramble Bush in 1853 (*a now disappeared dwelling near the site of present day Beech Lea in Trelessy Lane*).

Joseph died in Tenby in 1863 and Elizabeth married John Watts, a widower, whom she probably knew from Crunwear. John, a farm labourer, had moved to Crunwear in the late 1840s and was living in Ruelwall in 1851 with his first wife Sarah and their children. By 1881 Elizabeth and John were living in Lawrenny and Maria was working as a servant. When she became pregnant they took her in and Alfred Mason was born at their home. Maria went on to marry Henry Childs, a widowed labourer, and they lived the rest of their lives in Begelly and St Issells.

****

John James, Alfred's father-in-law, was the only child of William and Ann James and almost certainly adopted. The 1871 census describes his relation to his parents as 'nursing' and his mother would have been in her mid-50s when he was born around 1856-7.

William was farming 18 acres at Ciffig when John came along, but by 1871 he had given up the land and the family moved to Cabin, Marros. Thirty years earlier John and Ann had lived nearby, at Watergoch, south of Crunwear (*now known as 1 & 2 The Hawthorns*), and they may have maintained ties with the area.

John married Sarah Lewis in 1876 when they were both working as servants. Sarah seems to have left home by the age of 17 and may have spent time working as a dairymaid for a farmer at Carew before her marriage. John went on to work as a labourer on farms and roads. Sarah became the village midwife (*Llanteg Down the Years* p. 83) and it may be that she learned some of her skill from her grandmother 'Molly the Barrietts' who lived till Sarah was 13.

Elizabeth Ann, the first of John and Sarah's ten children was born at Coomshead, but by 1881 they were living at Ruelwall, where they would spend the rest of their lives surrounded by children and family. Sarah's widowed mother Eliza was already living with them and William and Ann James moved to nearby Ledgerland. John was present at his mother's death in 1883.

William James, remarkably, remarried the next year, and went on to have three children. His bride, Hannah Davies, was at least 30 years younger than him, and William knocked seven years or more off his age in the marriage certificate. They moved to his home town, Lampeter Velfrey, where he lived on into his nineties.

John James died in 1915 but Sarah lived on at Ruelwall another 16 years with her daughter Ellen and her husband Fred Allen. Her granddaughter Eileen was born in 1922, the fourth generation of the family to live in the house.

John and Sarah are buried in a corner of St Elidyr's churchyard, Crunwear. Sarah's death marks the end of a period of at least 150 years when my family lived and worked in Llanteg and its immediate surroundings. I'm struck by how rooted these people were and how many of them lived out their lives in the same community or within a very few miles of their birthplace.

I've been surprised and delighted at how much I have been able to find out about my ancestors and flesh them out as characters, and I'd like to thank Ruth Roberts, John Lewis-Tunster, Alan Mason, Owen Vaughan and Ted White as well as the Llanteg Local History Society for their help in my research. I'd welcome any further information which could add more detail to their lives.

The Mathias Family
by Ruth Roberts

Twins Lucy and George Mathias were baptised in November 1905, the children of John and Ann Mathias of Pendeilo. Ann was originally from Blackheath, the daughter of William and Mary Davies and granddaughter of James Davies and Jennet (née John).

The 1901 census shows the family at Lower (or Little) Pendeilo (with four rooms) - John 33 years and born at New Moat, Annie 34 years and born Crunwere, and a daughter Martha Anne aged 7 months, born in Amroth parish.

John was the son of Jonah Mathias, a farmer who was born in Maenclochog about 1846 and who spoke English and Welsh. John's mother was another Annie, who was also born in Maenclochog around 1838.

John and Anne married in October 1894. Their eldest son was William Edward who was born in 1902, dying in 1975. William married Phoebe Elizabeth (Cissie) Howells, the daughter of William and Catherine Howells, Little Ludchurch. William and Cissie had two children: Kathleen Ann and W.N.John. They moved from Pendeilo during the war to farm at Parcseison, near Princes Gate.

John died in 1917 aged 49 years and Annie had further heartache in 1918 when she lost her 14 year-old son and 38 year-old brother-in-law within 3 days. She was also to lose her daughter, Martha Ann (Pattie), in 1928 aged just 27 years. Annie herself lived to a ripe old age of 84 years, dying in 1951. They are all buried at Zoar, Llanteg.

In 1936 Lucy married Cyril Wilfred Evans, a farmer at Corner Park Farm, Reynalton, and had two sons – Geoffrey and Haydn.

George never married, and later lived with his cousins Mildred, Florence and Leslie (Lel) Phillips at Middleton. George died at Elidyr Cottage in 1967, the home of his other cousins, Herbert and Betty James, who had kindly looked after him during his final illness.

Some Ancestral Links to Crunwere
by David Walling

Two of my maternal great-grandparents were Henry (born 1827) and Ann Thomas of Temple Bar Cottage (and later Beulah Hill) in Amroth. Because Henry's niece was another great-grandmother he also happened to be my great-great-uncle. Henry had received some basic education at Lanteague Day School where Richard Davies was the school master. Jim Thomas recorded that Richard Davies was Henry's uncle, and I can only assume that it was through marriage, though I'm not exactly sure how.

Henry started work at the tender age of eight, working underground at Earwear Colliery (Amroth) and then at the iron ore quarry near Amroth Burrows. He had various jobs throughout his life at different collieries, ceasing work in 1900, at 73 years of age! In addition Henry was a Lay

Preacher and, though an Anglican, took more than 4000 services at local chapels, including preaching 244 times at Zoar Baptist Church and 566 times at the Congregational Church (*Mountain Chapel*), both in Llanteg.

When Henry was 22 years old he married Ann Drummond Davies at Crunwere on 5th April 1849. Ann was the daughter of James and Jane Davies of Broomylake, Llanteg, and she was over three years older than Henry, being born on 7th November 1823 at Frogsford (later called Oxford), near Crunwere Church (*now an empty cottage along the lane which passes the church field entrance*).

Jane Davies's mother (and Ann's grandmother) was Sarah Llewellyn (wife of Henry John whose large family tree is mentioned elsewhere in the book). According to James Thomas's notes Henry John, another of my great-great-grandparents, lived at Stanwell Villa (formerly known as Little Griggs) in Crunwere, where he was Clerk at Crunwere Church.

Ann was named Ann Drummond after a great friend of the family, Anne Drummond McIntyre.

Anne Drummond McIntyre was the daughter of Dr William McIntyre, and niece of Jane McIntyre who married a William Davies, a Welshman who had gone to Scotland as a member of the Welsh Regiment. They later returned to Wales and lived at Crunwere Farm. Ann McIntyre joined them there. Jane Johns was their maid. William Davies purchased Broomylake, and after the death of both William and Jane Davies the holding passed to their niece – Ann Drummond McIntyre.

In her childhood days Ann Davies also attended Lanteague Day School, an old building subsequently used as a Congregational Chapel and situated nearly opposite Crofty Nursery, near to and on the south side of the old turnpike road (*now completely disappeared – it was subsequently superseded by the 'new' Mountain Chapel which itself has now been demolished*). Ann was first taught by Mr Evans and then by Mr Rowlands. Like her future husband, Ann left school very young, spending her time assisting her mother, who kept three cows at Broomylake, working at harvest time and at other times working for Robert Morgan of Trenewydd. When she was about seventeen years old she lived for nearly a year at Great Craig y Borian, where Robert Morgan had engaged her as assistant dairy maid to Ishmael Rees and his wife Eliza. They lived in the old farm house (in ruins by 1906), near the pond on the eastern side of the modern house. They had rented the milk supply for £7 per cow per annum from Robert Morgan, who occupied the lands. At the time the 'modern' house was occupied by a

Scotsman, Mr Brown – later the house was much enlarged.

After this Ann remained at home for four years before going, in September 1845, to work at The Royal Oak Inn (now called Oaklands), to relieve her sister Jane, who was leaving to get married. The Inn was kept at that time by Thomas Voyle, the brother of Mrs Robert Morgan. Ann remained at The Royal Oak for thirteen months and whilst there she attended the wedding of Thomas Lewis, held at Sparrow's Nest in April 1846. Here she 'fell in with' Henry Thomas, and they courted for three years, during which time she lived at Crunwere Rectory for nine months and also assisted there at other times. From August 1847 to August 1848 Ann lived at Baglan and Aberavon Rectories, in the employment of Rev'd Richard Morgan and his family. Henry and Ann Thomas had seven children, the second son, Richard, being my grandfather. A younger son was James.

Ann died in November 1907, six years after Henry. There is no doubt of her son James's love and respect for his parents. Perhaps this is because he lived at home after a shunting accident on the railway which ended his working life and also his intended marriage. So his parents replaced any family of his own that he might have had. The challenges he subsequently took on, however, have provided a valuable family and local history record for future generations. It is to James Thomas that I owe much of my family information; but I am also grateful for information supplied by Ruth Roberts who herself turned out to be a distant cousin – for Ann Thomas's younger brother, William Davies, is Ruth's great-great-grandfather.

Mr Walling has done much more research into his family, especially the Amroth connections – if anyone thinks they are related and would like to get in touch, please contact the History Society.

The Family of John Allen Phelps
by Allen Phelps

My father John Garfield Phelps (known as Garfield) was born on the 15th January 1903. He was one of five children, having two brothers, William and Oliver, and two sisters, Susanna and Laura. Apart from Garfield, Oliver was the only one to have married but he had no children. They lived with their parents John and Mary Phelps (née Phillips) at No 1 Newton Terrace, Ryeland's Lane, Kilgetty (it was then called 'Hill 60').

My father left school at fourteen and went to work in Bonville Court

Colliery, Saundersfoot. In June 1928 he married a farmer's daughter from Llanteg, Eleanor Mary Allen (known as Nellie) - the daughter of John Henry Allen and Janet Elizabeth Allen of Rose Cottage - and they made their home in Begelly.

In May 1930 their daughter and my sister, Winifred Doreen (known as Doreen) was born and in September 1934 their son John Allen (myself) was born. In 1935 my family moved to Llanteg to live in a small cottage located near to Milton Farm called Milton Back, which is now a ruin. We lived there for twelve years before moving to the School House in Llanteg in 1947.

During World War II Garfield served with the R.A.F. Regiment. Unfortunately, after a short time he was discharged on medical grounds but was still able to serve an active part in the Home Guard. After the war we moved to the School House in Llanteg (now known as Sea Breeze) and during this time my mother (Nellie) was caretaker of the Church Hall (the Old School). In 1948 my father went to work at the Proof and Experimental Establishment (P. & E.E.) Pendine, where he remained until his sudden death on 24th December 1961 aged 58 years.

After my father's death my mother remained in the School House until moving to Saundersfoot in 1975. My sister Doreen married Melvyn Gwyn Evans in 1956 and they made their home in Ludchurch. They had five children: Vicki, Paul, David, Nigel and Siân. In 1969 they moved to Atherstone, Warwickshire, where they set up in business as funeral directors.

In 1994 my mother went to live with her daughter Doreen and family in Atherstone where she died in 1996 aged 94 years. Both Eleanor and Garfield are laid to rest at Crunwere Church at Llanteg. Doreen died in May 2005 aged 74 years. Melvyn died in December 2008 aged 83. They are both buried in Atherstone where they had made their home for the last 40 years.

I was educated at Crunwere School, Llanteg, until the age of 12. The school, with only 11 pupils remaining, was eventually closed and I moved to Amroth School in 1946, leaving school in 1949. In 1951 I commenced an engineering apprenticeship at the P. & E.E. Pendine and in 1953 was transferred to Liverpool. I completed my apprenticeship in September 1955 to become an Engineering Craftsman. I spent two years in the R.A.F. doing National Service and was stationed in Wellsbourne near Stratford-Upon-Avon. Afterwards I worked in Liverpool for two years before returning to Llanteg and employment at the P. & E.E.

Pendine. I was employed as an Engineer and stayed in this employment until my retirement 38 years later in 1997.

In October 1963 I married Barbara Reynolds from Pendine, where we made our home. In May 1966 our daughter, Nicola Joanne Phelps, was born, followed in January 1968 by our son, Kevin John Phelps. Nicola married Meurig Williams, a Police Officer from Tenby, in May 1992 and they have two daughters, Rachel, born 1996, and Lucy, born 2001.

After teaching in Bridgend for a number of years Kevin met and eventually married a teacher from Cardiff, Olga Psaila (of Greek descent). They married in 1997 and moved back to Llanteg in 2002. They have two sons, Toby John Phelps (born 1998) and Joseph Andreas Phelps (born 2000). They built Surfhaven in Llanteg in 2002 and have lived there ever since. In October 2007 Kevin was appointed Head Teacher of Tavernspite C.P.School.

The Wilkins Family of Amroth and Crunwere
by Ruth Roberts

Unconfirmed information from the internet shows that a James Wilkins married Hester/Esther Reynolds in Eglwys Cummin in 1836 and their son John Wilkin was christened in Eglwys Cummin in 1844.

The 1851 census shows James, 35yrs and born Llanddowror, and Esther (39) living at Marros village with three children – Thomas (11), John (7) and Mary (5). James gave his occupation as cabinet maker.

By the 1861 census James and Hester Wilkins had moved to Castle Ely and were living there with their sons Thomas (22, also a cabinet maker), John (16) and daughter Mary (14).

In 1871 the family were just over the stream from Llanteg – living at Honeypot Hill, Marros parish. John now had a family of his own – with wife Ann (26yrs and born in Amroth) and children Ester (6), William (4) and Susan (2).

The 1871 census shows John's parents, James and Esther (both 55) living at Croft Cottage, Marros, with their daughter Mary, son-in-law John Thomas and two grandchildren, James and Thomas.

By 1881 James Wilkins had died and Hester is shown as a 72 year old pauper, still at Croft Cottage Marros, with just her grandson James Thomas, who, at 14, was a farm servant.

John Wilkins and his family had moved to Amroth by 1881 when they were shown living at Steps. John and his wife Ann were both shown as being born in Amroth and aged 37yrs with their children Susanna (12yrs born Ciffig), Jennet (9yrs born Amroth), Mary A. (7yrs born Amroth), Sarah (5yrs born Amroth) and James (2yrs born Amroth).

In the 1891 census for Amroth we find the Wilkins family living in a two roomed cottage, Castle Bach. John Wilkins, aged 46, was the head of the household with his wife Ann, also 46 years. With them were five of their children: Esther (25yrs), Sarah (14yrs), James (12yrs), Thomas (9yrs) and John (4yrs). Also living with them were three grandchildren: Martha Elizabeth (6yrs), Margaret (3yrs), and David (2 months). From the Baptism register I have been able to find out that Margaret and David were Esther's children.

By the time of the 1901 census the family had moved to Skerry Back (which was shown as two rooms). John Wilkins, aged 56 years, now gives his place of birth as Marros and his occupation as a 'labourer in wood' (possibly working on the Colby Lodge Estate, or following in his father's footsteps as a carpenter). Also there were his wife Ann (56) and three of his children: Esther (35, a washerwoman), Sarah (24) and John (who at 14 was described as a Post Boy). There were also three grandsons: David (10yrs) Thomas (5yrs) and Oliver (1yr) - Thomas being the son of Mary Ann Wilkins, Esther's sister.

The Roll of Honour for 1914-18 in Amroth Church mentions three of the Wilkins family:

T.Wilkins M.M.	Gunner	R.G.A.	France & Belgium	
J. Wilkins	Driver	R.A.S.C.	Salonica	
David Wilkins		Corporal 2nd Wilts Regt Belgium		Killed in Action

The award of a Military Medal to 371167 Gunner T.Wilkins R.G.A. (Amroth) was published on the 25 September 1917. Family tradition has it that he was the last man with a large gun on the field in France. Tom lost his hearing as a result of World War One and it was many years before he had a hearing aid and was able to hear the birds again.

It is believed that 8204 Corporal David Wilkins was killed in action on Saturday 24th October 1914 somewhere in Belgium and has no known grave. His name appears with 54,000 others on the Menin Gate, Ypres, Belgium.

Mr Tom Wilkins M.M. married Gladys Phillips of Middleton, Crunwere. The marriage took place in Crunwere in 1933 when they were both 37 years old. Tom was then living at Kilanow Gate and had put on the register that his deceased father had been John Wilkins (who had actually been his grandfather). Tom was a gardener and he later went on to be head gardener at Llanmiloe House, Pendine. Tom and Gladys were to make their home at Sandy Grove, Llanteg. The Narberth Weekly News of 11th May 1933 records a 'Pretty Crunwere Wedding' between Mr Thomas Wilkins of Amroth and Gladys Mary Phillips, eldest daughter of Mrs and the late Mr T.Phillips, Middleton. The bridesmaid was Miss Millie Phillips (sister of the bride), the duties of best man being ably carried out by Mr Albert Wilkins (cousin of the groom). The bride, who was given away by her brother, Mr Tom Phillips, was 'neatly attired in a brown crepe suede dress, with hat to match. On leaving the church the happy couple was showered with confetti by a host of well wishers'. The reception was held at Middleton and they received 'a large number of useful presents'.

Tom was given a clock for his time at P. & E. E. Pendine.

He had been offered a job at Hyde Park but his wife Gladys had not wanted to move. He was a very knowledgeable gardener and would do wreaths for funerals and also wedding flowers. He won lots of prizes for his fruit and vegetables at shows (and so did other people!)

His nephew Elvet now has his gardening diary. Often at weekends Tom would visit Elvet at Summerhill, travelling down by bus. They would possibly go for a pint at The Commercial pub (*now a private house near Kilanow Cross*) and then have a lift home.

Gladys and Tom had one little baby who sadly died. Tom had plans for improving Sandy Grove but these were abandoned when Gladys died in 1955. Tom continued to live there alone until his death in 1969.

In Tom's will were bequests of £50 each to Margaret, Kathleen, Gillian and Alan: 'to the children of Mr & Mrs Davies, Trenewydd, for their kindness and company which they gave me during my last years of life'. Also bequeathed was £25 each to both Crunwere and Amroth churches, as well as three willow dishes, an oak chest of drawers and three butcher's knives to Elvet.

Henry John and his Descendants
by Ruth Roberts

Henry John was born in Amroth Parish c1750 and married Sarah Llewellyn in October 1780. She was also of Amroth, born around 1757. When I was researching my family tree I managed to get back as far as Henry John with the help of Ted White of Canada. Ted was researching his wife's family who are also descended from Henry John's son – another Henry! However Ted had been unable to find documentary evidence that the younger Henry was actually the son of this Henry John.

It would be a few more years before Henry John's Will was found with the help of Owen Vaughan. This Will proved conclusively that Henry John did indeed have a son who was also called Henry – thus confirming Ted White's researches.

Henry John died in October 1822 and his Will shows him as being 'of Longlands, Crounwear'. We later found from the old Deeds of Zoar Chapel that this probably was what is called The Griggs today – as the land which was given for the building of the chapel was also called 'Longlands'.

Henry's Will lists bequests to his children:-

Son Thomas – 2s 6d
Son Henry – 2s 6d
Daughter Sarah – 2s 6d
Daughter Genet – 2s 6d
Daughter Ann – 2s 6d
Daughter Maretta – 2s 6d

Henry willed to each of the daughters named above 'the best room in his dwelling house called Longlands with a good bed and also a fire to sit by when sick or sore or cannot follow their daily labour, while they remain single and not married, during the term of the leasehold'. And to his beloved wife Sarah John, the leasehold dwelling of Longland with his money, goods and chattels. Sarah was to be the Executor and the Will was witnessed by Thomas Dalton (Minister), James Dalton and James Lewis.

You may think that would have been the end of the matter, but we then found another line who traced themselves back to Henry John – from Philip Nicholas of Baglan.

Whilst conducting our researches as a History Group, John Lewis-Tunster began collecting the various family trees connected with Llanteg that we were finding, and loading them all into a large Family Tree programme on his computer. We gradually began to see that a large proportion of local family trees could somehow all find their way back to the union between Henry John and Sarah Llewellyn. Unfortunately we have been unable to get any further back.

John has now recorded 600+ descendants from the marriage of Henry John and Sarah Llewellyn – and this is only from four of their children – there are still three which we have not followed up yet!

Children of Henry & Sarah (with a few descendants shown):
Thomas (born c1783)
No descendants found as yet.
Henry (born c1784)
This line leads to Gaynor White (née Davies of Tenby) who now lives in Canada.
Sarah (born c1788)
This line leads to Philip Nicholas of Baglan.
Mary (born c1791)
Mary's line leads to the Lewis and Davies family trees which had connections with Ruelwall, Milton and Sparrows Nest.
Jenette/Janette/Jane (born c1794)
Leads to the Davies and Scourfield families which had connections with Blackheath, Middleton and Greenacre families.
Ann (born c1797)
No descendants found as yet.
Maretta (born c1808)
No descendants found as yet.

Other local families can trace themselves back as far, and further. However we believe that this family tree is the one which spreads out the furthest – as one lady commented "it has the most branches!".

Why all these lines should go back to just one couple is unclear, although there is probably a statistical reason that could explain it.

It really does seem to us that this couple really are the 'parents' of recent Llanteg. What happened before the 1750s we can only guess at – but as this couple were both born in Amroth parish it seems that whoever the original pre 1700 Llantegers were – it was not them.

If you have any family connections or family tree details that we have not been told about please get in touch. We can then add the information to our ever growing Village Family Tree and may also be able to add in a few of the missing pieces for you as well.

The Dalton Family – Royal Connections?
by Ruth Roberts

The Dalton Family Crest
Photo: Dalton Genealogical Society

We first became interested in finding out more about the Dalton family in September 2000 when a tomb was uncovered in St Peter's Church, Carmarthen, of Charlotte Augusta Catherine Dalton (died 1832 aged 27 years), and her niece Margaret Augusta Prytherch (died 1839 aged 8 years). They were supposedly the granddaughter and great-granddaughter of King George III and his first wife, Hannah Lightfoot. The then Prince of Wales had fallen in love with Hannah Lightfoot, a London Quaker girl and daughter of a London linen-draper, and married her in complete secrecy at Kew on the outskirts of London on 17th April, 1759. They went on to have three children. Two years later in 1761, George, now King, married Charlotte Sophia of Mecklenburg-Strelitz who became his Queen.

One of the King's daughters by Hannah, Sarah Catherine Augusta Ritso, married a James Dalton of Carmarthen, a Doctor and Officer of the East India Company. They in turn had two daughters, Charlotte Augusta Catherine and Caroline Georgina Catherine (who was the mother of Margaret Augusta) and two sons - Henry Augustus and Hawkins Augustus.

Now the clue to this Sarah Catherine Augustus and the naming patterns of all four children that have the same name of Augustus must tell us something of the truth of Sarah being a daughter of King George III, or as he was known then as George, Prince of Wales. King George's mother was Princess Augusta of Saxe-Gotha and he named one of his sons Edward Augustus.

We therefore decided to trace the family of a Llanteg resident, **Graham Mortimer** (whose grandmother had been a Dalton) to see if we could find any connections.

Taking Graham and his sister Donna to be the **1st generation** we traced them backwards as follows:-

2nd Generation – their parents were John (Jack) Stephen Mortimer and Ayah (née Phillips).

3rd Generation – **Graham** and Donna's paternal grandmother was **Elizabeth Dalton** (wife to Thomas Henry Warlow Mortimer).

*Elizabeth Mortimer
(née Dalton)*

Photo: Ashley Burland

Elizabeth was born in Eglwys Cummin parish around 1872, the youngest daughter of **John** and Margaret **Dalton**. Elizabeth's mother died when she was a baby and she was brought up by her aunt at Summerbrook, Llanteg. Her aunt had also been born Elizabeth Dalton and had married Evan James of Marros. John and Margaret Dalton had the following children: William (born 1861), Mary (1864 – possibly working at Llanstephan shop in the 1881 census), Caroline (1866), John (1867) and Margaret (born 1869 and who later lived at Blaenhafod, Crunwere, until her death in 1947).

4th Generation – **John Dalton** had been born in 1837 and at the age of four was living at The Norton, Llanteg, with his family. This property has now disappeared but was situated south-west of the present Llanteg

Garage. John's parents were **William Dalton** and Mary (née Scourfield), and he had a younger sister Elizabeth (born in 1840 – it was she who later raised John's daughter Elizabeth), and a younger brother David (born 1845). John married Margaret and farmed in Eglwys Cummin parish (he was shown at Ivy Cottage on the 1881 census and at Rose Cottage in 1891). However both he and his wife are buried at Crunwere Church and their grave is marked by an obelisk (John died in 1908 aged 70 years and Margaret died in 1873 aged just 44 years, shortly after her daughter Elizabeth's birth).

5th Generation – John's father **William Dalton,** was born in Crunwere in 1811 and married Mary Scourfield in 1840 (she had been born in 1806 at Lampeter Velfrey). William had at least two sisters, Elizabeth (who later married John Watts of Eglwys Cummin) and Martha (who married Allen Palmer and went on to run the Golden Lion Inn, Llanteg, later to change its name to The Laurels). William was a road labourer and had the task of maintaining the road to Tavernspite (*Ben Price article 1924*). William and Mary are also buried at Crunwere Church, Mary dying in 1877 aged 69 years, and William dying in 1888 aged 77 years. They had also lived at The Norton.

6th Generation – William's father was **James Dalton,** born circa 1770. He was classed as 'Gent' on his daughter's marriage certificate but 'farmer' on William's and is shown on the 1841 census as receiving an Army Pension (Rodney Dalton believes he may have been in the Royal Navy).

It is evident now that we may be confused with the number of James and Thomas Daltons in the area at that time. Neither myself, Ashley Burland nor Rodney Dalton have been able to clarify the situation before going to print. However we have still included the information from the 7th Generation back as all the Welsh Daltons sprang from the same roots and it makes very interesting reading. Hopefully we may unravel the dilemma soon.

7th Generation – James's father was **Thomas Dalton**, born circa 1751 and who became the Vicar of St Issells from 1782 until his death in 1839, and was also Vicar of Crunwere from 1783 until 1830. A plaque inside Crunwere Church records his family as: Anne wife of T.Dalton Rector 29/1/1815 aged 76 years also daughter Elizabeth 26/5/1818 aged 41 years also son John Gent Surgeon 26/5/1822 aged 41 years.

(Researcher O.J.Vaughan note: Suggest Thomas Dalton of Rhos Crowther is the eldest son of Thomas Dalton born circa 1751.)

8th Generation – Thomas Dalton's father is believed to have been another **Thomas,** the Vicar of Fishguard, who had three siblings. Thomas Dalton senior was the third son of **Edward Dalton** and was born in 1714 at Gower, Glamorgan.

9th Generation – Edward Dalton was the fifth son of **James Dalton** and Joyce (née Vaughan) and was born in 1685 at Pembrey. James had escaped, at the age of one year, with his family after the Battle of Worcester in 1651 when the Daltons had fought for the Royalists.

10th Generation – James Dalton had been born in 1650, the second of two surviving children of **Walter Dalton III** and Jane (née Needham).

11th Generation – Walter Dalton III lived from 1603 to 1666. He played an active part in the Civil War. Living near Witney in Oxfordshire, he fought for the Royalists in the regiment of his cousin, Colonel Thomas (Lord of the Manors of Thurnham, Cockersand and Bulk from 1626: Colonel Thomas Dalton of Thurnham raised at his own expense a regiment of horse, with which he served in the Royal Army in the Civil War, and died of wounds received at the second battle of Newbury, 1644). Not deterred by Cromwell's victory and the death of the King, he joined the invading Scottish army led by Charles II. A family tradition is that either he was the paymaster of the Army or he was associated with that office. With Walter went his younger brothers Charles (1605–1651) and William (1614–1651), together with other relatives and friends. The Scots and their supporters proved no match for the military genius of Cromwell and the Royalist Army was routed at the Battle of Worcester in September 1651. The fight was an exceedingly bloody business even by Civil War standards and many Royalists were killed, including both of Walter's brothers. According to one source 'at this battle there were ten Dalton brothers, cousins and uncles killed'. A verbal family tradition has it that Walter, and a relative called Roland, managed to escape the battlefield, laden with the Royal Paychest. The tradition is also emphatic that the Battle of Worcester was the great calamity which befell the family. Walter hastily collected his wife and young children and they began to make their getaway to South Wales. The journey lasted into the winter of 1651 and the conditions were so harsh that three of Walter's children died – Thomas aged 8, Ormonde aged 6 and Walter aged 3. The youngest child, James, aged 1 year, survived to become the ancestor of the south Wales Daltons (known as the Junior Dalton Line) and also a branch of the family in Utah, America. Walter and his surviving family settled down at Pembrey near the seat of Golden Grove. His travelling companion had been Roland Vaughan, a cousin to the Earl of Carberry, Sir John Vaughan, who resided at Golden Grove.

Walter's financial position appears to have been satisfactory and he sent his son James to the Inns of Court in London where he qualified as a Barrister-at-Law. James, probably through both his Vaughan and Dalton connections, acquired the post of Receiver for the Duchy of Lancaster, which was later held by his eldest son John.

It is obvious that the Civil War had a devastating effect on Walter and his family. The number of male Daltons was drastically reduced and the young James Dalton's chances of survival could not have been rated high in the hard winter of 1651. Yet the family adapted, survived and rebuilt both its numbers and its socio-economic position – quite a remarkable feat in the troubled period of British history. Walter's son James went on to marry Joyce, the daughter of Rowland Vaughan, who had escaped with him from the battle field, thus uniting the Vaughan and Dalton families.

12th Generation - Walter Dalton 11 of Curbridge, Witney, 1582-1605/7?

13th Generation - Walter Dalton 1 of Curbridge, Witney, 1552-1619.

(Family tradition has it that money from the sale of Curbridge was given into His Majesty's own hand by Walter Dalton, in a long leather purse, at the top of the stairs at Christchurch, Oxford, and land was bought in Wales with the residue.)

Information still to be proved has the Daltons descended from Sir Rychard Dalton of 'Byspham in Lancashyre', born around 1230, who was himself descended from Le Sieur de Dalton who came from Normandy with King Henry II in 1153.

So where was the connection between our Graham Mortimer and the supposedly royal graves in St Peter's Church, Carmarthen? As far as we can tell if you look at the 8th generation above – Thomas Dalton senior (third son of Edward Dalton, Graham's 5x grandfather) would have been first cousin to the James Dalton who was married to Catherine Augusta and the father of Charlotte Augusta Catherine whose tomb was uncovered in 2000.

(With thanks to Graham Mortimer, his late sister Donna Burland and nephew Ashley Burland for supplying recent information on the Dalton family, and to Alun Lloyd Davies, webmaster of St Peter's Church, Carmarthen, for information on the recent grave discoveries. We are also indebted to Mr Rodney Dalton of Utah, USA, and the Dalton Genealogical Society for providing information from Rev'd Thomas Dalton of Crunwere back to Walter Dalton of Witney born 1603.)

Mr Rodney Dalton can trace his family line back through another Thomas Dalton who was born in 1731 and who emigrated to America around 1760. He was the great-grandson of James Dalton, born 1650, from whom all the Pembrokeshire Daltons appear to be descended. Mr Dalton is writing a book about his line of Daltons of whom the first was Sieur de Dalton of Normandy, France, born about 1125 AD.

If anyone has any additional information on the Dalton family and its descendants, both Llanteg History Society and Mr Rodney Dalton would be delighted to hear from them.

The George Family of The Downs
by Ken George

Kenneth George

Richard George married Elizabeth Oriel at Narberth Registry Office on the 21st February 1889. Richard was shown as being 21 years old and coming from Llanshipping/Martletwy, with his father also being called Richard and classed as a mason. Richard junior was shown as a farm labourer on the marriage certificate but he had learnt his trade as a mason with his father from the age of eleven when he was working on chimneys as a steeple-jack (most collieries had these large chimneys in those days). After the colliery accident at Landshipping he moved into farming, working at Manor Court Farm, Pendine – it must have been whilst working here that he met his future wife, whose address was given as Marros.

Richard George junior was born at Backs Wood Cottages, Landshipping, and also tried farming for a while at Upper Castle Ely Farm before moving to The Downs, Llanteg.

The 1891 census for Cyffig shows the family residing at Castle Ely, just over the parish boundary from Crunwere – Richard and Elizabeth George were living with their one year-old daughter Martha who had been born in Cyffig parish (*she later married William Hendry James from Bevlin and lived at Manchester House, Tavernspite*). Unfortunately Richard's occupation was blank.

By the 1901 census the George family had moved to The Downs, Llanteg. Richard's occupation was shown as a 'timberman underground' and he was living with his wife Elizabeth and their three children: Martha, 11 years, born at Cyffig, Richard, 5 years, born at Eglwys Cymmin (*Gwilym Richard later lived at Templeton*) and Elizabeth, aged 3 years and also born at Eglwys Cymmin (*always known as Ginnie*). Another son, Melville, died on Christmas Day 1902 aged just 3 months. In 1903 Richard and Elizabeth had a third son, Arthur.

Elizabeth George died in 1922 aged 58 years, whilst Richard lived until 1958, dying in May aged 90 years.

Arthur lived at The Downs, and married Sarah Anna Lloyd. They had six children: Kenneth 1929, Clifford 1932, David 1936, Mary 1938, Winifred 1940 and William (Billy) 1945. Arthur farmed The Downs all his life, retiring to a little bungalow (Hillcrest) on land at his farm. Sarah Anna died in 1981 aged 76 years, followed less than five months later by Arthur, aged 78 years – they are buried together in Crunwere churchyard.

(Researcher O.J.Vaughan note: Richard George aged 12, a scholar born at Llangwm is shown as the son of Richard aged 64 born at Burton and Martha George aged 40 born at Llangwm residing at Baxwood, Martletwy, Pembrokeshire in 1881. Elizabeth was the possible daughter of John and Martha Oriel of Churchen Cottage St Issells. Elizabeth Oriel was probably a servant at the home of Mary Palmer, Farmer at Parky Nock Farm Laugharne in 1881. A tantalising alternative is that Elizabeth Oriel was in fact Elizabeth Pirt who was shown as the adopted

daughter of William and Sarah Oriel in 1871- this would also account for no Elizabeth Oriel being listed in Civil Registration for 1866. Whilst Elizabeth in 1881 maintained she was born at Marros, it is far more likely she was born at Neath, where her parents had married in the Neath Registry Office. That this is in fact Elizabeth Pirt (née Oriel) then the adoption theory is further supported by the fact that a John Oriel was also at Parky Nock Farm in 1881 and since there is currently no known location for John Oriel, the son of William and Sarah Oriel in 1881, an acceptable solution is resolved.)

Daniel and Jane/Jennett Griffiths of Crunwear
(now known as Llanteg)
by Helen Williams (née Griffiths)

Daniel Griffiths was the third son of William and Francis and had been baptised in Lampeter Velfrey on 10th February 1805, William being the village blacksmith. It is believed (though not established) that his eldest brother William junior (born c1800) became a tailor who went on to live first at Trenewydd Lodge and later at Sandy Grove, Llanteg.

Daniel and Jane are my great-great-grandparents. They married in Lampeter Velfrey Church on 23 February 1829, with both making their mark rather than signing their names. Jane's name variously appears on censuses as Jane, Jennet, Jennett and Jenate.

They had at least six children:- Margaret c1829, Elizabeth c1831, John c1840, Jane/Jennett c1845, Frances c1847, and William junior c1850.

Their first two children were born in Crunwear, Pembrokeshire, indicating that Daniel moved to Crunwear from Lampeter Velfrey to live with Jane soon after their wedding in 1829. However in 1840 their third child John was born in nearby Cyffig, Carmarthenshire, and the 1841 Wales census shows Daniel as blacksmith there.

By the time of the 1851 census Daniel and his family had moved back again to Crunwear, to a property known as Crafty (also known as Crafty Corner and Crofty). Today, this property is known as Crofty Nursery, Llanteg.

Crafty seems originally to have been composed of outbuildings, two dwellings and 16 acres. Local history records refer to a small school being held there for a while in the mid-1800s. The 1841 census shows the head of household at Crafty as Elizabeth Davies (75), a dealer in fish - she does not appear on the census again, so probably died during that decade.

The 1851 census shows Daniel as a blacksmith farming ten acres at Crafty, and as Jane's maiden name was Davies it looks as though Jane and Daniel moved back to Crunwear to take over the property when Elizabeth Davies died. It might be worthwhile to check old property and Will records for the parish. Books published by Llanteg Local History Society mention Daniel and his family, and also contain photos of them. He can also be found in local trade directories.

Throughout the 1850s and 1860s the second house at Crafty was occupied by John Davies and his family, an agricultural labourer occupying 6 acres. John Davies is possibly the man named as 'Johnny the Welshman up at Crafty' by Ben Price in his newspaper articles and reminiscences.

Local history records suggest that people from Lampeter Velfrey were often Welsh speakers, unlike those from Crunwear. This anomaly probably stems from the time of the Norman occupation when Lampeter Velfrey was placed in the Welsh enclosure and Crunwear in the English. Daniel is recorded on the 1891 census as speaking both Welsh and English - there is every possibility therefore that his parents, siblings and wife, were also Welsh speakers. He was popularly known in Crunwear as 'Dai Crafty'.

Jane and Daniel remained at Crafty until their respective deaths in 1888 and 1893. They are both buried at St Elidyr's Church, Crunwear.

Bishop's Transcripts record Daniel and Jane's third child John as having been buried in Crunwear aged 13 on 29th June 1853. However, Pembrokeshire Record Office state that none of their children appear to have been buried there, and John is not listed on the index of Crunwear Grave Inscriptions produced by Llanteg Local History Society. To date I have not managed to obtain a copy of his death certificate because the index reference number is indecipherable and his name is very common - I am still working on this. In the year of John's burial there were apparently far more deaths than usual in Crunwear, so errors in recording might well have occurred. He does not appear on the 1861 census, but as he would have been 20 by then it is theoretically possible that he could have been alive and living elsewhere.

Daniel and Jane's daughter Elizabeth was born about 1833 and on the 1861 census she is shown as unmarried and still living at Crafty with her family. Her occupation then was given as servant. At the age of about thirty-five she gave birth to an illegitimate child (Elizabeth Jane

Griffiths) who was brought up at Crafty by Daniel and Jane.

Some time between her baby's birth on 20th May 1868 and the next census in 1871 Elizabeth disappeared, and to date I have not been able to locate her. There is no record of death for her around this time, so perhaps she married and/or left the area. My aunt recalls a family story of her having moved with her employers to Pimlico, where she rose to the position of housekeeper in their household and was briefly married to a soldier who was subsequently killed on active service.

There is a mystery surrounding the formal registration of Elizabeth Jane's birth on 2nd June 1868. The baby's baptism record (5th July 1868, Crunwere) names Elizabeth as the baby's mother, whereas the birth certificate states the mother to be Jennett Griffiths. Elizabeth does not feature anywhere on her daughter's birth certificate and the father's name has been left blank. The birth was registered by one Jennett Griffiths, who made her mark rather than signed her name.

Given the obvious difficulties of hiding the later stages of any pregnancy and the fact that the baby was born at Crafty in the middle of the family's own tight-knit community, the baptism records probably reflect the truth of the matter. It seems that either Elizabeth's sister or mother (both Jane/Jennett Griffiths) misrepresented the facts to the registrar when registering the baby's birth in Narberth. Given the evidence on the certificate of making a mark rather than signing, the most likely culprit is Daniel's wife Jane - even though her age (63) would have stretched the boundary of credulity to its limit! My father once described our ancient Pembrokeshire relatives to me as having been anarchic by nature, but we shall never know for certain whether this was a deliberate act of deception or merely a simple error.

Elizabeth's baby, Elizabeth Jane, remained at Crafty with her grandparents even after marriage. She and her husband Joseph Phillips of Middleton took over the property after Daniel and Jane had died. They had twelve children in total, two of whom died as infants in 1894/ 95 (bronchitis and whooping cough). These children are all listed (with some photos) in the Llanteg Local History Society book entitled *Llanteg - Turning Back the Clock* (2002, p. 80). I think that these children and/ or their children might have been the relatives that my father and aunt were regularly taken to visit 'somewhere near Tenby'.

The picture below was taken in Swansea c.1900. It is of William Griffiths and his wife, Elizabeth, with their four children (L. to R: Naomi, George Henry, Florrie, Thomas Daniel).
William was the youngest child of Daniel and Jane Griffiths of Crafty. William and Elizabeth were my great-grandparents. Their youngest child, George Henry, was my grandfather.

Photo: Helen Williams

Daniel and Jane's youngest child William (c1850) worked alongside his father as blacksmith at Crafty before moving to Swansea in the early 1870s to become an enginesmith/fitter. William settled there and married Elizabeth Lewis, the daughter of a local blacksmith. They had four children, the youngest of whom was my grandfather George Henry Griffiths (born 1894), a marine engineer. William was secretive and feisty by nature – 'a person with attitude', as my aunt remembers him.

My grandfather George Henry Griffiths married Beatrice Richardson in Swansea. They had two children - my father George Henry Griffiths junior (1916-2008) and my aunt Elizabeth (Betty) Lewis (born 1918), who still lives today in the same Swansea street where she was born.

My aunt tells me that after William moved to Swansea around 1872 he used to take his children back to visit Daniel and Jane at Crafty once a year until Jane's death in 1888. This involved catching a train to Whitland station and an epic walk across the fields to Crunwear, stopping off for a cuppa at various dwellings along the way in order to rest my grandfather's poor little legs. The Phillips family at Wiseman's Bridge were a regular port of call. On one of these occasions my grandfather took a shine to a baby piglet and wanted to take it home with him. The mighty tantrum that he threw on being refused is the stuff of legend!

My aunt remembers being taken on regular visits to William's sister Frances (Fanny) Lewis née Griffiths who had several children and lived at The Folly. As an adult, right up until the late 1940s she used to go from Swansea on the back of a motorbike to visit Fanny's unmarried daughter Mary Lewis in Kilgetty. Mary moved there from The Folly to look after the children of one of her brothers, who had been widowed.

The Jenkins Family of Lanteague
by Ruth Roberts and Sue Blake

On the 1841 census John Jenkins was living on his own with a Bridget Jenkins aged 25 - possibly his daughter?

By the 1851 census the family were at Lanteague (William's father John was shown as a gardener aged 74 who had been born in Ludchurch).

On the 1861 census the family were at Little Bounty (*a now disappeared dwelling along the Crosslands Road*):-

Father - William 42 years (no place of birth shown)
Mother - Harriet 45 years (born at Narberth)
John 12 – born Crunwere
James 12 – born Crunwere
Margaret 10 – born Crunwere
Mary Ann 9 – born Crunwere
Elizabeth 8 – born Crunwere
Elena 6 – born Crunwere
Bridget 4 – born Crunwere
William 10 weeks – born Crunwere.

Margaret was not with the family on 1871 census.

In 1891 the Jenkins family consisted of:-
William – a carpenter

Harriet
John – a mason/builder
Ann – general servant.
The 1901 census shows:-
Harriet - widow 84 years
Ellen - daughter
Emily- grandaughter (born Twyford Middx).
The John who was 12 in the 1861 census could have been John Jenkins of Lanteague, a 55 year-old mason who died 3 January 1900. The verdict of an inquest into his death, held on 5th January at Lanteague Farm, was 'found drowned but how drowned there is not sufficient evidence to show'.

Margaret Jenkins is Sue Blake's great-grandmother. She married Walter William Platford on June 11th 1874 at All Saints church, Boyne Hill (district of Maidenhead, Berkshire). According to the marriage certificate she was a servant at the time of her marriage and Walter was a stonemason. Her father's name on the marriage certificate is given as William and she put down his profession as carpenter.

She and Walter had 12 children: Cecily, William Walter, Ellen Harriet, Charles Frederick, Margaret, Ada, Beatrice Lucy, James, Florence Emily (Sue Blake's grandmother), Robert Arthur, Gertrude Anne, Mabel Elizabeth - all were born in the Maidenhead area.

Walter died on 4th March 1901 in Maidenhead aged 52. Margaret died on 5th September 1917 in Maidenhead, aged 68.

The Lewis family of Homeleigh and Coombs Farm
by Greg Lewis

The story of my ancestors in Red Roses appears to be a tale of two farms.

My dad, Clive Lewis, was born at Homeleigh Farm in September 1938. His parents were John Lewis and Winifred Jane Lewis (née Thomas), and he had an older brother, Brian. John had been born in Oaklands, Llanteg, on December 27, 1894.

According to John's obituary notice: 'During his early life he was on the teaching staff of Tremoilet School, Pendine; he also qualified under the London Secretaries' Association... He was Clerk to Eglwyscumming (*sic*) Parish Council for ten years and was a lay-reader and an active church worker at different periods at Eglwyscummin and Crunwere Parish Churches'.

The London Secretaries' Association was an association made up of representatives from different Protestant churches which oversaw missionary work. My dad said that he believes John also spent time training as a barrister at Sear Green, near High Wycombe. However John returned to his father's farm to help out and ended up a farmer at Homeleigh.

He was a keen cricketer, rolling his own cigarettes behind the stumps, and between 12 June 1940 and 31 December 1944 was a member of the Home Guard. A citation from the King recalls that, 'In the years when our Country was in mortal danger (John Lewis) gave generously of his time and powers to make himself ready for her defence by force of arms and with his life if need be'.

Homeleigh took in some Italian prisoners-of-war, too. They worked on the farm and were friendly to the young Clive. My father remembers two, Elmo and Carlo, with much fondness.

John Lewis appears in *Llanteg Down The Years* as the chair of a Temperance meeting in February 1927 when the Narberth Weekly News noted his 'excellent address' to those in attendance.

John's obituary (I have the cutting but not the name of the newspaper) records that his 'death cast a gloom over a wide area, as he was well-liked for his quiet and unassuming disposition'.

My dad joined the RAF as a boy entrant in 1954 and when his father died on 2 April 1959, aged 65, Homeleigh left the family. John Lewis had three sisters: Morwen, Rowena and Tilly.

The other farm in the tale, Combe or Coombs Farm, has a connection through Morwen, as I understand she lived there with her husband Evan Richards.

It appears that John Lewis himself had grown up at Coombs. At the time of the 1901 census, John Lewis, my grandfather (whom I sadly never got to meet), was just seven. He appears on the census as a scholar living with his family in 'Eglwys Cymmyn' (a place spelt a dozen different ways by census takers through the years) at an address referred to simply as 'Coombs'.

At the time, the family consisted of John's father Thomas, a 35-year-old farmer and employer, and mother Mary, aged 33 and born in Llanboidy; a second son named Cecil, aged five, and two daughters, Mathilda (Tilly), aged three, and Margaret, aged two. There were two servants in the household - John Yea, aged 20, a Taunton-born carter, and Martha Wilkins, aged 16, a general servant, from Amroth.

My dad remembers the Coombs Farm of his childhood (at the time of the Second World War) as being a milk farm of about 70 acres. Homeleigh, where he grew up, was smaller, about 47 acres.

Looking back to the 1871 census, John's father himself was just a child. Thomas Ebsworth Lewis was aged six and living in Eglwys Cymmyn with his own father, another John, and mother Mary. This John was a labourer. John and Mary are my dad's great-grandfather and great-grandmother. Also in the house at this time were Thomas's sisters Mary, aged 16, Bridget, aged 13, Martha, aged 10, and Margrett (*sic*), aged two. Thomas was the fourth child of the couple. All had been born in Eglwys Cymmyn. Their address in 1871 was given just as Red Roses. Neighbouring addresses were 'Pig in gate' and 'Red Roses'. John was 45 at the time of the census and his birthplace was given here as Pendine. Mary was 42, and both she and her eldest daughter Mary had no occupations. The three middle children were at school.

It was the 1851 census which gave me information about the previous generation. At that time, John, my dad's great-grandfather, who had been born around 1825 or 1826, was a farmer still living in Eglwys Cymmyn – not with his wife, but with his mother. She was listed as 50 year-old Brigett (*sic*) Hodge, who was 50, having been born around the turn of the 18th-19th centuries. Brigett – my own great-great-great-grandmother - is a mystery. She not only brings one new and intriguing surname into the family – Hodge – but at least two others. You see, she ran a busy household – there is no husband listed on the 1851 census and she is listed as the head of the household. As well as John, then 25, the house provided shelter for his 21 year-old farming brother William Lewis; two other youngsters described as Brigett's sons, Thomas Harries, aged 17, and Robert Hodge, aged 12, and still at school; plus Brigett's daughter Sarah James, aged 21, and her own daughter, also Sarah, aged three months. There was also a dairy maid named Elizabeth Lloyd, aged 16, from Laugharne. Brigett had quite a little empire, referred to on the census as or at Cryfettan. She is shown as a farmer with 155 acres and three labourers. The whole family was described as Pendine-born, except the new addition, little Sarah, who was born in 'Eglwyscumin'. This document is intriguing. It appears to suggest the following: that Brigett had a son (John Lewis) when she was about 25, followed by a second son (William Lewis) four years later. Her daughter, Sarah James, was born at the same time. The James surname here is perhaps easy to explain. She had at birth, I assume, been a Lewis but had married a Mr James. Her husband is not on the census but it does confirm she was married. Their daughter had his surname too, of course.

However, it is not so easy to explain the different surnames of Brigett's other children. Her fourth child, who came along four years after William and Sarah, when Brigett was about 33, was called Thomas Harries. Did this child come from a second husband? A man named Harries? Then, five years later, when she was aged about 38, Brigett had a fifth child, Robert Hodge. Did this child come from a third husband? We have to assume so, seeing as Hodge – at the time of the 1851 census - is now Brigett's surname. So, had Brigett lost two, possibly three, husbands between the age of 25 and 38 – a man named Lewis (from whom my family name now survives), a man named Harries and another named Hodge? It seems possible. It is also possible the third of these, Mr Hodge, was still alive in 1851: although he makes no appearance on the census and Brigett is listed as the head of house, she is also described as married. Just those few scrawled entries in a census suggest Brigett was a fascinating character.

Did she inherit her land from a husband or a parent? Was it the land which made her such a good catch or was it (as I like to think) her formidable personality? Were multiple marriages usual in 19th century Red Roses? Or is there some other explanation?

Because my father never really returned to Red Roses after leaving the RAF, information on the family is scarce. His mother, Winifred Jane Thomas, was from Narberth. She had been born at Mountain View, Station Road, on 6 November 1908, and like her brother Albert she became a teacher. She died on 4 June 1987, aged 79 years. Her father, Lewis Watkins Thomas, was born on March 22, 1874, at Castle Inn, Narberth, where his father William was the innkeeper.

I set off on my initial family tree quest by looking at my mother's (*Laugharne**) side of the family, but I had help there: a family Bible and small box of documents.

This information on the Lewis family has been largely gleaned from internet searches (I wonder what Brigett would have made of Google) and no matter how powerful a tool that has become, it does not have all the answers. But it does leave you with an awful lot of questions.
*There is also a family link here through the Harry family of Laugharne with Ruth Roberts.

58

John Henry Martin – The Trenewydd Connection
The Last Survivor of Captain Cook's
Third Voyage of Exploration
by Peter Preece

In the graveyard of St Elydir's Church, Ludchurch, is the well preserved tomb of John Henry Martin, a naval man whose greatest claim to fame was that he sailed with Captain James Cook on his last voyage of exploration.

It was on May 6th 1776 that Martin, then aged 23, joined HMS Discovery as an able seaman. The Discovery had been chosen by Captain Cook as support vessel to HMS Resolution for his third voyage of exploration, the chief objective of which was to find a North West passage that would connect the Atlantic and Pacific Oceans. After little more than three months Martin was rated midshipman. Throughout the four-year voyage Martin apparently carried out his duties diligently and properly, but without distinction. He fired muskets when required to deter the advances of threatening natives, and he dealt out punishments to crew members for misdemeanours. By 1795 Martin is recorded as serving as First Lieutenant on HMS Syren. It is believed that Commander Martin retired from the Navy in 1801 on completion of 25 years service.

But what has any of this to do with a little book about Llanteg?

Well my own interest stems from the fact that I have lived at Martin's Farm, Templeton, which is named after Commander Martin and his family, from 1985 to 2006.

On tracing the Martin family I found that in 1802 records show that John Henry Martin married Ann(e) Ormond, widow, at St Peter's, Carmarthen. Ann was shown as being from Crunwere. They set up home at Trenewydd, a substantial farm on the outskirts of Llanteg, where Ann had lived with her former husband, David Ormond. This is confirmed by the Land Tax Assessment papers which in 1802 show Ann Ormond as the occupier of Trenewydd, but by 1810 the occupier was shown as Captain J.H.Martin.

I believe that Martin's connections with Templeton began at Trenewydd because on November 1st 1785, Ann Martin's first husband, David Ormond, had surrendered a mortgage, property details of which included 'messuages and lands called Woodside and Roadside, and closes called Towns End and Townred, all in Narberth'. Templeton was then part of Narberth South, and to this day has a Woodside and Roadside.

It is known that John and Ann Martin had a son who was baptised privately in Crunwere on August 1st 1803. This son was named Harry, but, as private baptisms were usually conducted at home soon after birth because of the sickly nature of the baby, it is not known if Harry survived.

Possibly he did, for later records show John and Ann Martin's son as Henry Owen Martin, Gent, solicitor, clerk to the magistrates, property owner and tenant farmer, in Templeton, Narberth. No other baptism records have been found.

It is believed that Ann Martin died in 1811 and that John Henry Martin remarried soon afterwards. His second wife was Margaret Thomas and she was a native of Cilymaenllwyd, Carmarthenshire.

Between 1811 and 1823 there is no information concerning the family's whereabouts, but in 1823 the following obituary appeared in The Gentleman's Magazine:

May 7th. At Narberth. John Henry Martin Esq RN.

He was, we believe, the last surviving companion of Captain Cook in his Voyage round the Globe.

Buried May 10th 1823, aged 70.

Martin was buried in the graveyard of St Elidyr's Church, Ludchurch. Even if he had lived at Templeton before his death he would still have been buried here. St John's Church, Templeton, was not built until 1839 and Templeton was previously served by St Elidyr as a traditional part of Narberth South.

To find the link between Martin and Templeton we have to go back to a family named Howells which also featured in the early ownership of Trenewydd Farm, Llanteg (*see also the 1686 Inventory of R.Howells earlier in this book*). Some time before 1785 this family mortgaged land in Templeton to John Ormond, the property being known as 'Howells Land'.

There is a date stone on the front of Martin's Farm that would strongly suggest that renovation works were carried out in 1783. I say *renovations* because it is believed locally that there was a house/dwelling on this site long before 1783 -

BUILT
BY H.H. sn
1783

In 1786 Howells Land was owned by Thomas Mancel, but by 1831 the occupier was Henry Owen Martin, the owner being John Hensley Allen of Cresselly.

An 1838 Picton Estate document also records that Henry Owen Martin of Templeton, Gent, leased for life from Sir R.B.P.Philipps of Picton Castle, three Templeton fields – Morris Hays, Pembroke's Acres and Pedlar's Park.

Margaret Martin, the Captain's widow, and her stepson, certainly lived at Howells Land for many years. Their occupancy is recorded in 1831 and although Margaret died in the 1860s, Henry Owen Martin was still living there at the time of the 1881 census.

Because of the long occupancy of the Martin family, the name 'Howells Land' eventually changed to 'Martin's Land', and in due course, to 'Martin's Farm'.

One key question remains – did Commander Martin himself ever live at Martin's Farm? To date the answer is 'not known', or possibly 'not proven'. But in any event Captain Cook's sailing companion still also had a strong connection with Templeton and Llanteg.

During recent renovations the new owners of Martin's Farm found two empty Quinine Bitters bottles embedded in the walls of the property. One use of quinine was to treat malaria – was this a relic from Martin's time?

We have also been in contact with John Curtis and John Sorotos of the 1805 Club which cares for the memorials of the Georgian sailing navy, and also Elizabeth Thomas, Churchwarden at Ludchurch.

Above the altar in St Elidyr's is 'a quite pleasing stained glass window apparently dedicated to the latter's (Henry Owen Martin's) memory by the then and newly elected Bishop of Llandaff'.

*John Curtis can confirm from the muster book of the bomb vessel **Explosion** that Martin was definitely in command of her during the battle of Copenhagen, 2 April 1801.*

This article was condensed and updated from one originally published in *Pembrokeshire Life* June 2003.

Ancestors of John Mason, Ruelwall
by Carol and Alan Mason

John Mason

Photo: Alan Mason

James Edgar John Mason was born 3 September 1920. He was called John, and was 18 years old on the day war was declared in 1939. John married Winifred Mabel Eileen Allen in 1942 and they lived at Ruel Wall Farm, Llanteg. They had two children - David Alan and Barbara Ann. John's parents were William and Catherine. William Mason was born in 1898, (dying aged just 43 on 20 June 1941), and his father, John Mason senior, is believed to have come from the London area. Catherine Mary (née Scourfield) was born in Carew in 1896. William and Catherine married on the 25th Oct 1919, William being a farm labourer at Knowles Farm, Lawrenny, and Catherine - also a farm labourer - living at The Grove, Cresselly. They were living at Hoarstone, Lawrenny, when John was born, later moving to Flower Hall, near Templeton. John had a sister, Annie Mary Elizabeth Mason (1923-1971), and brothers Dennis George Roberts Mason (born 1929) and David William Mason (1932–2005). Catherine Mary later lived in Rose Cottage, near Narberth, and died aged 69 in 1965.

Catherine's parents were James Rodgers Scourfield (1856-1926) and Mary Anne Gough (1867- 1960) born in Carew. The family later lived in Cresselly. Mary Ann, aged 87 years, was pictured in the local newspaper with her great-great-grandchild showing five generations of family members. Mary Ann's father James Gough was born in 1827 in Clonmel in Tipperary, Ireland. He married Catherine Scourfield (born

1830) in Carew. They married in 1855 - the censuses from 1861 to 1901 show the family living in Carew. James was a stone mason working in the quarry in Carew Newton, and Catherine a dressmaker. Catherine's parents were David Scourfield (1799-1888) and Elizabeth Rees (1798-1873) who were married on 1 Nov 1823 in Cosheston. David was a limestone quarryman working and living in Carew Newton. David's parents were David Scourfield (1766-1840) and Catherine Thomas (1763-1857).

Catherine Mary Mason
(née Scourfield)
with her mother,
Mary Ann Scourfield
(née Gough)

Photo: Alan Mason

Five generations of family members:
Sitting: 87 year old Mrs. M. Scourfield, The Croft, Cresselly.
On her knee, 3 month old Marlene Elizabeth Hughes (her great-great-grand-daughter).
Left is the baby's great-grandmother, Mrs. J. Harries, grandfather William Harries of Carew and mother, Mrs. Doreen Hughes of Slebech.

Photo: Alan Mason

John Mason worked at Trecwn, and for Wimpey at Templeton Airfield before being called up for War service in 1943. In January 1944 he was promoted from Stoker to Stoker 1st Class. John was 23 years old when he was killed on 14 June during the Normandy invasions in 1944. Stoker Mason, on Landing Barge Oil No 6, sailed with the 34th landing barge flotilla from Poole in Dorset, heading for the American UTAH beach in Normandy. Records show that on the 14 June a Stoker was lost, with no known grave. John Mason appears to have been the only casualty on that barge. John Mason is remembered on the Chatham Naval Memorial in Kent. John's widow Eileen (Oriel) unveiled a Memorial Tapestry in Llanteg Hall in 2004. Eileen Oriel (née Allen and later Mason) was born at Ruel Wall Farm, 18 Nov 1922 and died 25 Oct 2008 aged 85.

John and Eileen Mason had two children - son David Alan Mason (called Alan), who married Caroline (née Callnon) and they have a son Andrew and now live at Carlands, Llanteg; and a daughter Barbara Ann who married Arthur Howells, and they have a daughter Margaret and a son Roger, and live at Blaenwaun, Whitland.

James Merrilees of Stanwell - 1890s
by Darryl Gwynne
Darryl is a descendant of Mr Merrilees and lives in Canada.
James Merrilees was my great-great-great-grandfather. The paper trail started with my grandparents Sidney and Edith Gwynne (married in Monkton Church, Pembrokeshire, in 1925). Sid's father was William Gwynne (born 1870) Monkton. On the marriage certificate of Sid's paternal grandfather James Gwynne (he married Sarah Lewis at the Pembroke Register Office in 1862), James listed James Merrilees, steward (occupation) as his father. I had originally interpreted the entry on the certificate as 'James Merrylap', but the fact that this surname does not exist led me to re-examine the writing and to see that the last part of the surname consisted of 'ss' not 'p' (in old handwriting, the leading 's' was like a backward lower-case 'f'), i.e. 'James Merryless' (confirmed by Bettye Kirkwood and Sylvia Birch who are familiar with old handwriting styles). James Gwynne's mother - single mum Mary Gwynne - must have named her son after his father. Interestingly, however, James retained his mother's surname. Thus I inherit my surname from 3x great-grandmother Mary but of course my paternal lineage is with Merrilees.

This connection has now been fully confirmed in a genetic

comparison of my Y chromosome DNA with that of Merrilees males worldwide. The Merrilees had a pretty much full family tree worked out years ago that included James Merrilees of Whitland Abbey (I attended the Merrilees Clan Reunion in Dunedin, New Zealand, last year!) showing the connection between the Merrilees of East Lothian, Scotland, and our James of Llanteg. The genetic analysis has now examined 37 genetic loci on the Y chromosome and I have a virtually perfect match with other Merrilees males.

According to the entry on the marriage certificate of James Gwynne his father was James Merrilees. James Gwynne was probably named after his father and the surname Merrilees was exceedingly rare in Wales. The names James Merrilees, the occupation as steward, and an analysis, matching my Y chromosome with other male descendants of James Merrilees's paternal grandfather makes it certain that I have the right man as father to James Gwynne. Scotsman James Merrilees (the only Merrilees in the South Wales censuses of the time) was steward to the Hon. W.H.Yelverston of Whitland Abbey. There seems little doubt that James Merrilees abandoned his lover Mary Gwynne. He was across the channel in Bristol in 1841, when she and her two children had already been confined to the Pembroke Workhouse where she died a year later. James was back in the Pembrokeshire - Camarthenshire border area by 1851. It seems very unlikely that James would have been rejected as a husband by Mary or her family; he had a good career and was from a respectable family in Scotland so it is almost certain that Mary's parents, Thomas and Hannah Gwynne, would have wanted him to 'do the right thing' and marry their daughter.

In May 2007 I followed the trail of James Merrilees and his ancestry, starting in West Wales and ending in East Lothian, Scotland. James turns up in the 1851 and 1861 censuses as the steward (person responsible for the day-to-day running of the estate) for the household of the Honourable William Henry Yelverton, former Member of Parliament and resident of the Victorian house at the ruins of Whitland Abbey. The Abbey House is located in Carmarthenshire near the Pembrokeshire border, just a few miles south of the Castell Dwyran area where Thomas Gwynne was born. William, a wealthy Irishman, had acquired the estate through his marriage to Lucy Morgan. Gillian Parker, owner of Whitland Abbey House, gave me a tour around the estate and showed me documents pertaining to Whitland history. The original Abbey (one of many ruined following the dissolution of monasteries by Henry VIII in the 1500s) was the main Cistercian House in West Wales and identified with the national aspirations of the Welsh people and princes (monks had settled at Whitland in 1151 under the patronage of Rhys Ap Gruffydd) (*Terence James Manuscript*).

James Merrilees apparently had become relatively wealthy by about 1870 - probably from a paternal inheritance - as by the 1871 census he had moved to his own property, Thane Cottage, just a short distance into Pembrokeshire in Amroth parish, where he was a farmer of 21 acres. In the 1870s he had moved north again (back toward Whitland) to Stanwell Villa, Llanteg, in Crunwear parish, Pembrokeshire (*Llanteg: Turning Back the Clock*), where his acreage had increased by seven (1881 census). In 1871 and 1881 James lived with his servant, Elizabeth Davies, a milkmaid who was about 10 years his elder. Following that he lived alone, and remained a bachelor. James lived at Stanwell Villa from at least 1881, through 1891 to the end of his life in 1896. All censuses list his birthplace as Scotland and the 1851 sheet gives a more specific location as East Lothian (just east of Edinburgh). James Merrilees outlived his son James Gwynne by about three years. Stanwell Villa still stands near the village of Llanteg. Stanwell was originally a two-storey cottage in the front with a single storey at the rear which gave two upstairs bedrooms at the front. It was the Brinsden family, who, around the mid-1950s, enlarged it to a four bedroom house by building up the rear of the house to make that into two storeys. James Merrilees died of natural causes at Stanwell Villa aged 85 on 14 March 1896. According to death certificate information, an inquest was held two days later. Such an occurrence did not necessarily indicate suspicious circumstances; it could mean that the coroner needed more information relating to the cause. For example if a doctor has not seen the deceased or could not determine cause of death then a post-mortem took place which may result in an inquest. An inquest might also be called if a death occurred away from home or out in public. James Merrilees died a wealthy man. He owned seven properties, and left five pounds to each of his tenants, 'who shall not be in arrears with their respective rents'. He also bequeathed charitable legacies to Sunday Schools for 'Bible teaching and no other purpose' (for many years he was superintendent of Sunday Schools in Amroth: see gravestone information below). James Merrilees left Stanwell to his grand-nephew with the strange proviso 'that he change his name to Merrilees within

12 months' and should reside at Stanwell. This proviso appears to have been overcome however, as the property was sold by 1911.

For his own lasting monument James left 30 pounds for a tombstone made from 'Scotch red granite' (*Llanteg: Turning Back The Clock*).

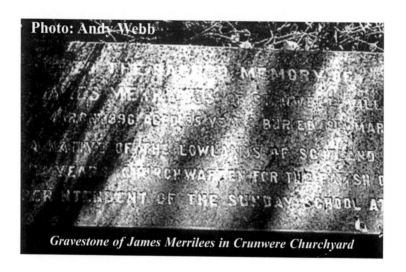
Photo: Andy Webb

Gravestone of James Merrilees in Crunwere Churchyard

The large red gravestone is still in excellent condition sheltered by trees on the east side of the Crunwere churchyard, and reads:

To the Sacred Memory of
James Merrilees of Stanwell Villa
Died 14th March 1896 aged 85 years. Buried 18th March 1896
He was a native of the lowlands of Scotland and was
for many years churchwarden for the parish of Amroth
and Superintendent of the Sunday school at Amroth
Honour thy father and thy mother that thy
days may be long in the land that the
Lord God giveth thee
1891 From The Mirage.
Even Now a Halo Lingers Over
Those Hallowed New Born Spheres
Gathering the Heart's Best Treasures Home
And Longing for a World to Come.

Frances Morgan – First Welsh Female Doctor and
The Llanteg Connection
by Ruth Roberts

The Morgan Family - In our third history book *Llanteg – Turning Back The Clock*, Judith Lloyd wrote of the Morgan family from Trenewydd:- 'By the 1820s Trenewydd had passed into the ownership of the Morgan family who were to be connected with the property for the next 40-odd years, beginning with Richard Morgan'.

After Richard Morgan's death his son Robert took over the farm, and the 1841 census showed him living there with his wife Elizabeth, daughters Elizabeth and Jane and young son Robert junior. Robert Morgan later moved with his wife and daughter Jane to Oaklands, an adjoining farm of 40 acres, where he died in 1847. Mrs Morgan continued here with her daughter whilst her son Robert took over the larger Trenewydd. The 1851 census describes Robert as a Registrar, lime merchant, and farmer of 480 acres - all at the age of 26 years.

His elder brother Richard studied at Jesus College, Oxford, and subsequently entered the Church. He became vicar of Aberavon and Baglan, dying of typhoid and pneumonia in 1851 aged just 42 years, leaving a widow, Georgiana (née Philipps) and five children. The eldest child was **Frances Elizabeth,** born in December 1843 at what is now 19 High Street, Brecon. The widowed Georgiana eventually returned to Llanteg and lived at Heatherland. She was a member of the prominent Philipps family of Cwmgwili, Carmarthen, and sister of Captain Lloyd Rice Philipps who for many years lived with his family at Oaklands, Llanteg.

By 1881 the Morgans had left Trenewydd. Captain Philipps's son Herbert moved from Oaklands to work for his aunt at Heatherland (the 1891 census shows him as a 'steward'), later marrying his cousin Catherina Sarah Morgan. After Catherina's death Herbert became curate of a little parish at Crickadarn, north of Brecon. They are both buried in the family grave in Crunwere churchyard, Llanteg.

Frances Elizabeth Morgan – was born on 20th December 1843 and went on to become not only the first British woman to receive a doctorate in medicine from a university in Europe, but also the first Welsh woman whose name appears in the British medical registers.

Frances obtained her medical degree from Zurich University in 1870 after three years' training - while also taking a course in Sanskrit. She graduated in 1870 with the distinction of being only the second woman in Europe to do so (the first had graduated from Zurich three years earlier).

Frances Morgan
(later, Hoggan)
as a girl

Photograph taken by
J.H.Goldie of Swansea
Photo: Roger Ford
(great-great-grandson
of Frances)

Frances married Dr George Hoggan in 1874 at Marylebone Registry Office (an unusual choice for the daughter of a church minister). She later practised in London as a specialist in women's and children's diseases. She became a campaigner and social reformer, and lectured in America. She had a particular interest in racial issues, and was a speaker at the Universal Race Congress in London in 1911. In 1892 the Medical Directory listed her as at her mother's address, 'Heatherland, Begelly'. Frances died in February 1927 and her ashes were interred with those of her husband in an unmarked plot in Woking cemetery.

The Mysterious 'Elsie'/Elise – it is now clear that more than ten years prior to her marriage Frances gave birth to an illegitimate daughter, Elise. The 1881 census shows a 19 year-old 'Elsie' (*sic*) as George Hoggan's sister-in-law. However if this were the case, and the girl was indeed Frances's sister, their father Richard Morgan would already have been dead 11 years before 'Elsie's' birth, so could not possibly have fathered her. Elise was born in Brussels in October 1861. Her birth certificate names her father as a 'John Morgan' and mother as 'Georgina Philipps'.

Although Elise was raised as Georgiana's daughter there is evidence that Frances did not simply abandon her to Georgiana's care. Frances would have been only 17 years old when Elise was born. According to Onfel Thomas, Frances had been studying in Paris, and it seems more logical that she should have travelled to Brussels to give birth rather than her mother doing so.

Frances Hoggan, possibly at Heatherland

Photo: Roger Ford (great-great-grandson of Frances)

The 1871 census records Frances living with her mother 'Georgina' (*sic*) aged 50, and 'Elize', aged nine, described on the census as 'niece'. When Elise married John Evans both Georgiana and Frances were witnesses. In 1911 Elise and her husband emigrated to Canada, where there are descendants living to this day.

We are indebted to Professor Neil McIntyre, The Cymmrodorion Society and Y Brycheiniog for their help and also permission to quote from their publications.

Granny Gertrude and the Parsell Family of The Valley
by Jean Gardner

My grandmother, Gertrude Amelia Watts, was born into a farming family in February 1889 at Penycoed Farm, Ludchurch. She was the second child of seven. Her father Robert, the son of a blacksmith, had married her mother Teresa in 1884. Teresa was the granddaughter of Henry and Sarah Morgan, whose family had farmed the land at Penycoed for over 100 years. Village records show Abraham Morgan was at Penycoed in 1776 (the farm remained in the family until 1971).

Gertrude spent most of her young years helping her mother on the farm. On leaving home Gertrude secured a position as servant at Cranmore House, Radyr, on the outskirts of Cardiff. It was not long, however, given her housekeeping and cookery skills, that she was promoted to cook/housekeeper. Her host family were the Birds, and she remained loyal to them despite numerous other offers of employment. Gertrude remained at Radyr throughout the First World War, joining organisations to help the war effort, for which she was awarded the Order of the Red Triangle in 1919.

After the war Gertrude went back to Ludchurch and became cook/housekeeper at Gellihalog Farm and married her childhood sweetheart, George Parsell, who worked at the local quarry. They had one child, a daughter born at Abbeystream Cottage in August 1921 – Enid Watts Parsell – my mother. After a few years working at Blaencilcoed, George and Gertrude had saved enough and in 1923 they were able to make a deposit on the vacant Valley Farm, which they farmed happily until the end of their days.

My grandfather was born into an old Pembrokeshire family who had mined and farmed in and around Amroth since the 16th century (family records show them in the Amroth area in 1786 but more research needs to be done to discover when they came to Pembrokeshire). Grandfather George was a collier who worked in local mines and quarries. He was a natural baritone – but in later life suffered from pneumoconiosis so that even holding a small conversation became a herculean effort. He had said that some seams of coal were as narrow as 18 inches and you would have to lie on your side to dig them out – or else you would be working on your hands and knees in water.

Nothing ever went to waste in the neighbourhood and everyone helped one another. Grandfather never complained about his poor health nor the hardships and work involved in running the farm. We all had to work hard and be sure to make ends meet. The small holding was just over 26 acres and every inch was farmed by hand. Our fields were still ploughed and tilled by horse right up to grandfather's death in 1953. Cousin Patrick, who was seven years older than me, had to take on the lion's share of the chores; most of my jobs were fetching and carrying water, or running errands.

I was born at The Valley in November 1941. My father was away fighting with the 8th Army – The Desert Rats - in Africa. Mother gave birth in the middle of the night with the help of my grandmother and Nurse Greenslade of Sheepwalks Corner. Nurse Greenslade was the local midwife and attended most local births. She would be seen cycling furiously in the direction of the forthcoming event. Grandfather was in poor health by then, but, being the only one available, he had to harness Polly the horse to the trap in the middle of the night to fetch the nurse. It was a miserable, cold night and grandfather said "that's the fastest that maid ever attended a birth in this parish, the wheels on the trap glowed red all the way back to The Valley". All mother mentioned of the birth was "I'm not going through that again!", and true to her word she didn't!

Enid Howells (née Parsell) with daughter Jean

Photo: Jean Gardner

After the Second World War, with the help of my mother, grandmother and cousin Patrick (who had come to live with us in 1942), Grandfather George was able to struggle on farming until he died in 1953, when grandmother took over until 1957.

Grandfather or Patrick would often catch a few rabbits for the pot at weekends, but more often than not a few rabbits or a brace of birds would be given to my grandmother by the local rabbit-catcher or one of our neighbours. After cleaning, grandmother would hang them in the larder for a few days to tenderise. Any food that was not able to be smoked, salted or pickled had to be eaten up reasonably quickly.

To ensure that my grandmother never missed the service bus I had to go up and watch for it a full half-hour before it was due. Hardly any motorised traffic passed the farm then (*although this was the main Carmarthen – Tenby road*) and you would hear the bus coming long before you saw it. There were no regular stops along this stretch of road and you just put your hand out to stop the bus. When the buses first began, there were only two services a week – one to and from Tenby market on a Friday and one to Carmarthen market on a Wednesday. On those days the bus passed about 8am, when grandmother would put her wares ready to sell at the markets, then she would return home in the evening loaded up with the essential shopping for the week.

A prescription from the doctor or a visit to the chemist meant a walk to Kilgetty. Being such a long way it was quicker for me to go down the field and harness up Polly to our small trap. Whenever I went to Kilgetty I would have to run around the nearest neighbours to see if they had any errands which needed doing when I was there (they would also do the same for us). On these unscheduled trips I would often end up with a list of things to do. There was only one pharmacy and doctor and the nearest vet was at St Clears. Health care and 'cures' often came in the form of home-made brews that were handed down through the family. There was no National Health and doctors and vets had to be paid for out of the income gleaned from the land, which was not very much. To make ends meet every penny had to be watched. If none of her cures worked grandmother would send for Mrs Smith, the local Charmer, to try and charm away any pain etc. with a prayer, one of which was:-

Flee Tanteny Flee, Here we follow thee
We three maidens, we three shall
This Tanteny Quell
Ships here way not God's answer
Tanteny Bush send this man/woman well
From the crown of his head to the sole of his feet,
In the name of the Father, the Son and the Holy Ghost, Amen.
(This was to be repeated nine times.)

Grandfather kept most of his fruit bushes under nets to protect them from birds. By mid August, or as soon as the blackberries appeared, we would be out in the fields walking the hedgerows and gathering them up for jam. The Valley land was south-facing and well sheltered by the steep-sided wood at Craig y Borian Farm. Every spare moment would be used in gathering the fruit, not only for grandmother's recipes but also to sell at market. In September the elder fruit began to ripen. Gran expected us to pick as much as we could for her wine making and medicinal recipes. Patrick and I would often have to climb trees to reach the fruit. The best time to gather was in the late morning/early afternoon when the sun had dried up the dew. In those days in summer everyone in the family would be out foraging the hedges for strawberries, blackberries, crab apples, mushrooms, wild herbs etc., or any other edibles that could be used or sold.

Grandmother loved baking and set aside Tuesdays for making the bread and cakes. She would often say "kneading bread has a meditating effect that brings you closer to God" - and I firmly believe it does. Bread-making was part of the joys of being brought up in the country. Grandmother would make us take our clogs off at the door before being allowed into the kitchen for supper – this was the one meal where we all sat down together. After supper, when everything was cleared away, we would sit round the fire and discuss the day's news and any gossip that had come by way of passing neighbours. By the light of the oil lamps grandfather would read the newspaper while grandmother read aloud from the Bible, and mother and I would often be sewing or knitting.

My mother, who by then was divorced, struggled on alone until the farm was sold in 1962, when she left the area. The day The Valley was sold was one of the saddest days of my life – I was totally devastated by its loss – it contained all my childhood memories – for me it had been a magical enchanting place.

The Family of Rev'd William David Phillips of Crunwere
by Megan Crofts
Megan Crofts is a descendant of Moses Phillips, who belongs to another line of Rev'd Phillips's ancestors. What she has been able to unearth about her family provides a very interesting story indeed.
William Davies Phillips – 1805-1886
W.D.Phillips was born on 8 September 1805 in Haverfordwest, and baptised in January 1809.

He married Henrietta Elizabeth Jones of Carmarthen on 5 August 1841 at St Peter's and they went on to have seven children:

Thomas Jones Phillips, baptised 1842

John Charles Phillips   1844

Edel Arabella Phillips   1846

(Edel Arabella married James Moore, also a Clerk in Orders. They moved to Liverpool and had three children. After her husband's death Edel moved back to North Cliff, Tenby, and by 1881 was shown as a schoolmistress. She later married Gabriel Rowe in 1887 and by 1891 was living at and running the St Andrew's Boarding School at Tenby.)

Caroline Mary Phillips 1848

(Caroline Mary married William Garner who took over Crunwere Parish on the death of her father.)

William Harcourt Phillips   1851

(William Harcourt was a medical student.)

Richard Wilson Phillips   1852

(Richard Wilson became Rector of Pendine.)

Leslie Arnold Phillips   1856

(On the 1881 census Leslie Arnold was shown as an Oil Broker.)

In 1841 they were living at Cliff Cottage, Amroth, with two servants.

By 1851 William was at Crunwere Rectory with his wife, three children and four servants.

William died in 1886 and was buried at Crunwere Church. Henrietta died in 1893 and was also buried at Crunwere.

You might think that this is all very standard family history news but as we delve back into his family tree we unearth some interesting facts.

William was the son of Nathaniel Phillips of Haverfordwest and Rachel Davies of Nevern.

Nathaniel Phillips – 1761-1837

Nathaniel was also born in Haverfordwest, the second son of Samuel Levi Phillips and Dorothy Hood.

Nathaniel married Rachel Davies in 1802 at St Mary's, Haverfordwest, and they had three children – Caroline Jane 1803, William Davies 1805 and Charles Nathaniel Nathan 1807.

Nathaniel inherited the Haverfordwest Bank on the death of his father in 1812; he was made a Freeman of Haverfordwest and was Mayor in 1824.

Unfortunately the bank collapsed on 25th December 1825 (like many other country banks) and Nathaniel was declared bankrupt in 1826.

Megan has a copy of a placard, dated 1825, which spoke of the panic relating to local banks, which they called 'groundless panic'. There had been a run on the bank and they suspended payment.

Samuel Levi Phillips – 1728-1812

Samuel Levi Phillips was the son of Nathan Phillips and Edel and was born at Uhfeld, Germany in about 1728.

Samuel Levi Phillips and his younger brother Moses are thought to have arrived in Swansea in about 1742 with another Jew named David Michael. Samuel and Moses probably moved to Haverfordwest either in the late 1740s or early 1750s - they are said to have been jewellers. Both brothers were baptised Christians – Samuel in 1753 at St Thomas, Haverfordwest, and Moses in 1755 at St Mary, Haverfordwest.

Samuel married Dorothy Hood in 1753 and was made a Freeman of Haverfordwest and was Sheriff in 1763. They had six children: Elizabeth 1754, Philip 1755, Sarah 1757, Dorothy 1758, Nathaniel 1761 and John 1762.

Samuel married his second wife in 1763.

Samuel and his brother Moses founded the Haverfordwest Bank in 1783.

Samuel was naturalised by an Act of Parliament on 29 June 1804.

There are two accounts of how the two brothers arrived at Swansea. One states that the brothers arrived with David Michael and the other says that Nathaniel, their father, also arrived, and that he founded the bank – but it was Nathaniel, Samuel's son, who took over the bank after the deaths of Moses and Samuel.

Samuel's Will of 1811 shows the prosperity of the family. Among the bequests are included:-

Barley Mow house in Prendergast

3 Houses in Prendergast

His house in Bridge End (plus fields in Prendergast)

A leasehold house in Milford

£3000

6 houses in the parish of St Thomas, Haverfordwest

Leasehold house in Lambeth, Surrey.

Some other interesting people are connected with this family tree:

Rev'd William Davies Phillips's younger brother **Charles Nathaniel Phillips** is buried in South Park St Burial Ground, Calcutta, India - *'To the memory of Mr C.N.Phillips late surgeon of the Ship 'Victory' who* *drowned on the 12th May 1836'.* The announcement of his death states that Mr C.N.Phillips drowned whilst imprudently bathing alongside the ship Victory.

Margaretta Phillips married Walter Rudding Deverell. They moved to Charlottesville, Virginia, USA after their marriage where their eldest son Walter Howell Deverell was born. Walter Howell Deverell was a friend of Rossetti, the Pre-Raphaelite artist. Walter used Elizabeth Siddell as his model for Viola in his painting 'Twelfth Night'. Walter died of Bright's Disease in 1854 aged 26 years and Dante Gabriel Rossetti used Elizabeth as his model for many of his famous paintings. Elizabeth was also the model for Sir John Everett Millais's painting 'Ophelia'. There are several drawings of Walter's brothers and sisters by Rossetti and Walter himself on view on the internet.

Elizabeth Phillips Hughes – there is still a Hughes Hall at Cambridge University, named after Elizabeth.

Sarah Phillips (daughter of Samuel Levi Phillips) married David Charles the famous hymn writer – his brother Thomas Charles was known as 'Thomas of Bala'. An account of David Charles states that his wife was the descendant of a famous Rabbi from Frankfurt who left Germany because of persecution.

John Humphries Davies of Cwrt Mawr was Principal of Aberystwyth University. He left his vast collection of books and manuscripts to the National Library of Wales as long as it was built in Aberystwyth.

David Davies – M.P. for Monmouth.

William Davies - Welsh tennis player.

One branch of the family is mentioned in Burke's Landed Gentry – **Gordon Alexander Phillips** of Adelaide, Australia, who was made a Freeman of Haverfordwest in 1907. He traces his Coat of Arms back to Sir Benjamin Travell Phillips who was in the Yeoman of the Guard.

The Purser Family - On the Trail of the Lost Hair Bracelet
by Ruth Roberts

While researching Llanteg village history we ordered a copy of the Will of Mrs Anne Jane Purser, a widow who lived at Llanteglos and who had died in 1903. The Will, worth over £1 million at today's value, was interesting in regard to its detailed lists of jewellery and other items (given in full in our previous history book *Llanteg - Turning Back The Clock*). However one item made us do a 'double take' as we read it:

In trust for Winifred Laura Purser – a hair bracelet with fastening containing Charles 1st's hair and monogram surmounted by the Royal Crown.

This hair bracelet aroused our curiosity, but as we knew nothing of the Purser ancestors or descendants, our search had begun.

We were fortunate in obtaining help and information from two unrelated sources. The first was from Mr Robert Stewart of London, who had coincidentally contacted our churchwarden regarding his own research into Pursers and their graves; the other was from the King Charles the Martyr Society, which Judith Lloyd had found on the internet, and who, in the person of Mr Jeffrey Monk, also became interested in our quest. It was Mr Monk's opinion that if the hair bracelet mentioned was genuine it would indeed be a unique find.

Thus began our task of tracking down as many Pursers in the records that we could find in an effort either to trace them back to find the family connection with Charles 1st or to trace their descendants down to the present day to see if the family still possessed the bracelet (because surely this would be something that would have been valued as an heirloom if it were genuine).

(Researcher O.J.Vaughan note - The first evidence of the Pursers comes from the Will of Henry Purser of 1663, a Husbandman residing at Bosherton. His Will made on 6 April 1661 was proven in the E.C.C. of St David's on 30 April 1663. Whilst his wife and son, Margarett and Henry Purser, were executors, Henry also makes reference to his five other children: sons Francis, John, William, and Rice Purser, plus his only apparent daughter Abra. Reference is also made to an unknown number of unidentified grandchildren who in 1661 were all minors. See following article by Owen J.Vaughan.)

The following Pursers found in the 1670 Hearth Tax returns are possibly the sons of Henry and are recorded as:-

Rice Purser	of Pwllcrochen Parish	- two hearths
William Burser *(sic)* of Stackpool		- one hearth
Henry Burser *(sic)* of Bosherton		- two hearths

First Generation – Our family line of Pursers can only definitely be traced at present as far back as George Purser who was born in 1747. George married Jane and lived at Morston Farm, Monkton. The Land Tax returns of 1786–1788 shows George Purser as being a tenant of two properties at Monkton - Morston and a large property called Goldborough. He was a Burgess and petty juror and had five children:

William (baptised 1782), Elizabeth (1787), George (1791), John (1798) and Francis (1804).

Second Generation – The eldest son William continued to live at Morston and married Dinah Gwyther of nearby Rhos Crowther in 1810. William was churchwarden at Monkton and went on to have the following children: Elizabeth (baptised 1812), Jane (1813), Thomas (1815), Dinah (1817), Mary (1820), Margaret (1823 who died aged 1 year), Margaret (1826 who died aged 3 years), and William George (1831). The family also lived at Fynnon Gain, New Moat, a farm of 132 acres which by 1873 was owned by W.G.Purser.

Third Generation – William and Dinah's eldest son Thomas married twice. His first wife was Sarah Elizabeth Stokes. She had been baptised at Wickwar in Gloucestershire in 1818 and was the daughter of a surgeon, Edward Stokes, who later lived at Manorbier and died in 1828 (he also had a brother, Thomas, who was a surgeon at New Milford). Thomas and Sarah married at Liverpool on 10 October 1854. The fact that Thomas was able to marry a surgeon's daughter suggests that the family were either already fairly well up the social ladder or that they were moving up the ranks. They appear to have had only one son, William Edward Purser, who was baptised in 1856. The family were at that time living at Craig-y-Borian, Amroth, with Sarah dying in 1870. When Thomas was 60 years old he married Jane de Villineuve, a 40 year-old widow, their marriage taking place in London in 1876. It was also Anne Jane's second marriage - she was born Anne Jane Jones in 1836, the daughter of John and Mary Jones of Carew. Thomas and his new wife continued to live at Craig-y-Borian, but by the 1891 census they had moved to Llanteglos in Crunwere parish. Thomas was to die in 1895 with Anne Jane following him in 1903.

Fourth Generation – Thomas's son by his first wife, William Edward, cannot be traced on the 1881 census (possibly he was out of the country, working in Australia). However by 1894 he is shown as a widower and Gent when he married Mary Anne Johns at Castell Dwyran Chapel (now derelict). William Edward was then living at Grondre, just north of Penblewin crossroads near Clynderwen.

William Edward had a daughter, Winifred Laura, who was born in 1894 to his first wife Laura Collins, and also the following children by his second wife: George Frederick (1895), Thomas Picton (1896), Cecilia Grace (1897), and Lucy Mary Elizabeth (1899). By the time of the 1901 census Mary Anne Purser was herself a widow and bringing up her family at Redstone Cottage, Narberth North. All the children were shown as being born at Grondre.

The Purser Family Group c.1899/1900
Mary Purser (née Jones) with stepdaughter Winnie (standing left)
and children George, Tom, Grace and Lucy (on lap)

Photo: Hilary Lestner

Fifth Generation – Winifred Laura Purser, the daughter of William Edward and Laura was born in 1894, the year of her mother's death. It was to her that Anne Jane Purser of Llanteglos willed the hair bracelet when she died in 1903. As Winifred Laura was still a minor, it was given to Rev'd Thomas David, Vicar of Llanddewi (*Velfrey?*) in trust.
The Relic
So how did the bracelet find its way into the Purser family? No one knows at present. However the Purser line that we are tracing shows that Thomas Purser of Llanteglos, Crunwere, was the eldest son of an eldest son (which is the line of descent that a valuable heirloom would follow). On Thomas's death the relic was in his second wife's possession, but in her Will she bequeathed it back to the Purser family (to Winifred Laura) who was the eldest daughter of Thomas's deceased son (the line

80

of descent therefore appears strong). Whether the bracelet continued its journey down through the years in Winifred Laura's family still remains to be seen.

We have now made contact with two relatives of the Llanteglos Pursers – Mrs Hilary Lestner of Lyme Regis and Mr David Purser in Australia, who have both been very helpful in our researches.

*Purser ring and brooch,
now in the possession of the Purser family in Australia*

Photo: David Purser

Mr Purser recalls his mother mentioning a lock of Charles 1's hair being in a mourning ring which he now possesses. Unfortunately the ring was altered when Mr Purser's uncle died in the Great War, when something was removed from the centre circle of black diamonds and a picture of the dead uncle inserted instead. The ring is inscribed 'Thomas Stokes Esq. died Jan 15th 1803 aged 70'.

However we believe that the story of the ring and bracelet may have become intertwined over the years as the 1903 Will specifically mentions both the hair bracelet and the mourning ring.

So although unable to trace the hair bracelet we have tracked down a ring containing hair. There is also a hair brooch still in the family – but no sign of the bracelet!

Follow up on the Pursers of Pembroke – Chasing the Hair Bracelet

Research, Composition and all errors by Owen J.Vaughan

Following hours of additional research concurrent with the information given in the article 'In search of the Bracelet' by Ruth Roberts on the Purser Family of Pembrokeshire, none of my research could be used because, although I could well see the connection, no definitive research actually linked the generations to the satisfaction of others. Like an itch that no matter how hard it is scratched, I could not put this failure behind me, I had to link these different generations of the Purser family. So setting my 'shoulder to the wheel', I decided the time had come to link my hours of unused research to the already known information. I may not show the generation's path of the hair bracelet but I was determined to carry the family back almost to the time of the death of Charles 1st.

In Ruth's article she clearly relates in the paragraph, Second Generation, the family back to William Purser, baptised at Pembroke 8 September 1783 of Moreston Farm, who married Dinah Gwyther in 1810 at Rhos Crowther. As Ruth so rightly says, their son Thomas Purser lived at Craig y Borion. From this agreed starting point we can overlap the marriage of George Purser of Moreston, father to William.

A solid connection which I had previously overlooked shows the son and daughter of William and Dinah living together in New Moat in 1881, but far more importantly, we have an uncle of independent means also living with them; he is George Purser aged 89:

1881 Census for Fynnongain, New Moat, Pembrokeshire

William G.Purser Head Unmarried 50 Monkton Farm of 350 Acres with 2 men and 2 boys

Dinah Purser Sister Unmarried 63 Monkton Housekeeper

George Purser Uncle Unmarried 89 Monkton Annuitant.

This now established my findings from the 1841 census which shows:

1841 Census for New Moat

William Purser	55	Farmer	Yes (born in County)
Dinah Purser	55		Yes (born in County)
George Purser	45		Yes (born in County)
Jane Purser	25		Yes (born in County)
Dinah Purser	20		Yes (born in County)
Mary Purser	15		Yes (born in County).

Clearly, not long after their marriage William and Dinah had moved from Moreston Farm up to New Moat and were probably already living at Fynnongain. The odd person living with William is George aged 45

82

Pwllcrochan Church and Moreston Farm, Pwllcrochan

Photos: Owen Vaughan

years, the assumption being he is probably a brother to William, whilst the three youngest are clearly known to be the children of William and Dinah.

Ruth had not been able to establish the spouse of George, but now I know it was Jane Williams of Popton (*in the Rhos Crowther area*). Now we start to establish the connection between my long hours of research and printed 'fact'. George, probably born circa 1747, was the son of John and Elizabeth Purser of Moreston Farm. Elizabeth (née Parry) resided and possibly was born at Castell Gwynne.

John and Elizabeth married circa 1730 had a sister Martha also of Moreston Farm who on 18 June 1730 married Benjamin Ferrier, born 18 January 1706. Following the birth of their son Samuel Ferrier, baptised 10 August 1732, Martha died and Benjamin married Jane Dunn on 30 December 1740. Their son Jenkin Ferrier, born 14 October 1741, married Mary Carrow on 3 May 1768. The Carrow family are also related to the Oriel family of Rhos Crowther and Pembroke Town during this same era, but as they say, the story of the Ferriers and Oriels (so dear to my heart) must await another time.

John Purser of Moreston Farm was born in the year 1710, the son of Francis Purser and Jane Bright, a couple who had married on 14 July 1702. I have difficulty with the actual number of children born to Francis and Jane. If, as seems possible, their daughter Jane was born in 1716 and died in 1729, then this couple had 13 children.

So having added another two generations and spreading the family to New Moat and incorporating the Pursers of Pembroke Town, can my research take us further?

One hook that genealogists cling to is the commonality in the use of Christian names in different generations - not scientific, but enough to lead most to connect the generations. In the Purser family of Moreston Farm, in their children at Pwllcrochan, Monkton and Pembroke, circa 1700-1730, we can discover such names as: Abra, Francis, Jane, John, Riecaus (Rees), not forgetting William and George. Turning to my long investigation and indexing of Wills we find: Henry Purser, who on 1 April 1661 was making his Will and living at Bosherton. In this Will we find Margaret, his wife, and his children, Abra, his daughter, and his sons Francis, John, Rike (Rees/Reece), Henry, and William. Needless to say, from the similarity between the names in the Will and future generations, Henry was beyond a shadow of doubt an ancestor to the Moreston Farm Pursers. Why no George in the Will? The popularity of the Christian name George would, I suggest, arise only with the House of Orange some 40+ years after Henry made his Will. Henry's Will was proven at the E.C.C. of St David's in 1663; thus deducing the approximate full age at marriage and 6 children (around 33 years) we can suggest he was born circa, if not before, 1630, and therefore was approaching his marriage at the death of Charles 1st in 1649, thus he was fully able to understand the events of the period. I often wonder as Henry wrote his Will in 1661 did he look back on his youth, when he perhaps answered the call of the Pembroke Town Bell, to defend Pembroke Castle with Laugharne and Poyer, or did he sit, possibly in the area of my own home overlooking the Castle, with the Cromwell forces laying siege to the Castle and town - but I digress. In 1717 an Abra Purser was baptised following her sister Jane's baptism in 1714. Some 57 years after Henry made his Will we find an Abra Purser marrying Saml. Harris of Pwllcrochan. Even later in 1770 we can find Jane Purser, probably baptised 30 January 1751 to John and Elizabeth Purser of Pwllcrochan becoming the second wife of William Oriel (son of Henry Oriel of Pembroke Town), the Excise/Customs Officer of Hubberston. Alas Jane only lived a further two years, when William then married Mary Mathias at Steyton. Continuing the commonality of surnames, we find Francis Purser at baptisms and marriages 1702–1734, Jane Purser 1716–1748, Elizabeth Purser 1712–1787, and John 1710–1760.

Henry Purser and family of Bosherton was not a 'one off' during the mid 17th century, as witnessed by the number of Pursers who litter the villages of the Castlemartin peninsula during the following centuries. So, whilst I cannot show how the bracelet appeared in the family, I hope I have satisfactorily added the missing generations between the 1750s and the significant year of 1649, and we are perhaps one more small step closer to finding out just how the hair of Charles 1st became a bracelet in the possession of the Purser family of Llanteg circa 1900.

The Scourfield Family
by the late George Vincent

I live in Port Talbot and my grandparents were George and Susannah Scourfield who lived at Milton Back, Llanteg *(now only ruins between Rose Cottage and Milton)*.

George and Susannah had nine children:-

Jack – who married Sally and went to live at The Cants, St Issells.

Jimmy – who died of meningitis after suffering a fall aged just 20

George and Susannah Scourfield
Photo: George Vincent

*Gwladys and Harriet Scourfield,
daughters of George and Susannah*
Photo: George Vincent

*Hugh and Hilda Scourfield
(children of Affie and Gwladys
Harris, née Scourfield)*
Photo: George Vincent

years when the family were living at The Moors. He is buried at Mountain Chapel.

Annie – who married Levi Jenkins, and who lived most of their lives at New Buildings, Sardis. They had a son Jimmy who served an apprenticeship at Ace's Garage, Tenby, before taking up life-long employment with the Bristol Aircraft Company. Their daughter Winnie continued to live at Sardis for the whole of her life and was a faithful member of Sardis Congregational Church.

Cissie – married Morgan Williams and had seven daughters. They lived at Velfrey Road, Whitland.

Gwladys – married Affie Harris and they farmed The Griggs. Their two children were Hilda and Hugh. Hilda was the organist at Crunwere Church for many years.

Rachel – married Tom Roberts, a railway worker. They lived at Glendale Terrace, Whitland, and had four children – George, Pattie, Lily and Ivy.

Harriet – married Bill, who was lost at sea. They had three children – Susie, Mary and Margaret. She lived at Lampeter Velfrey for most of her life.

Mary – married Tom Lewis and had two children – Hayden and Elsie. Both children became teachers. Hayden was popular in Whitland for all his civic work.

Lizzie – (Elizabeth), my mother, who married Harry Vincent, a steelworker. They had two sons – William and George (myself). Billy died very young of Saint Vitus's Dance. My parents met when my mother was in service with a local doctor at Penygroes. The doctor transferred my mother to Port Talbot. Prior to this my mother spent a period of time at Llanteglos, Llanteg. My father also died young, but my mother survived well into her nineties.

The Wilkin Family of Amroth and Crunwere
by Owen J. Vaughan

In 1801 the Wilkin family was resident in Crunwear living at Bowmans Pit (*a now disappeared dwelling*). It was here that David Wilkin resided and his Will proven by his executor and wife Margaret Wilkin. Other beneficiaries beside his wife were Margaret Scourfield, the daughter of Thomas Scourfield, Hannah William and Hester David (shown as sisters) and David Wilkin, son of the brother to the testator William Wilkin.

Prominent members of the community were witnesses, they being Thomas Dalton, vicar, Richard Llewhelling and Benjamin Phillips. The Wilkin family name remained in the village as shown by Griffith Wilkin when he voted in the 1831 elections.

20ᵀᴴ CENTURY CRUNWERE
SOME NOTES ON MOUNTAIN CHAPEL

(Taken from notebooks and papers found after Mrs Lilian Callnon's death and kindly lent to the History Society by her daughter Carol Mason. Mrs Callnon was Secretary and one of the last members of Lanteague Mountain Chapel when it closed in 1999)

annotated by Ruth Roberts

The first chapel had been formed in Bevlin field (east of present chapel yard) in 1814, and the present chapel (*before it was demolished*) had been built in 1889. A description is in our first history book: *Llanteg – Down The Years*.

On 10ᵗʰ August 1889 O.H.P.Scourfield signed over as a Deed of Gift, *'This plot of ground, half an acre in extent on Lanteague Mountain, now belonging to the farm of Oaklands in the parish of Crunwere in the county of Pembroke.*

'I Owen Henry Philipps Scourfield Bart of Williamston hereby give as a free gift to that society of Christians called Congregationalists now worshipping near the spot to them and their successors of the same faith and principles for ever to build a chapel on, to form a burial ground and to erect any buildings required for the convenience of worshippers thereat but for no other purpose whatever. Present Pastor - Lewis James, Deacons - Thomas Phillips and David Williams.'

A meeting was convened in March 1915 for the appointment of new Trustees. Rev'd John Howell Phillips of The Retreat, Amroth was the chairman.

The old continuing Trustee from 1889 was shown as David Williams of Trenewydd, farmer. The new Trustees chosen at the 1915 meeting were:-

Rev'd John Howell Phillips, The Retreat, Amroth Parish, Minister
Benjamin George Evans, Pendeilo Cottage, Amroth Parish, Gardener
Thomas John, Blaentydwell, Lampeter Velfrey Parish, Farmer
George Scourfield, The Griggs, Crunwere Parish, Farmer
John Callen, Cwmshead, Amroth Parish, Farmer
Thomas David Richards, Post Office, Amroth Parish, Grocer

William John, Green Villa, Ludchurch Parish, Labourer
Signed John Howell Phillips (chairman)
Hannah Williams, Long Lane (wife)
Gladys Scourfield, The Griggs (spinster)

In 1935 members and friends gave their labour and the materials for free when they coloured the chapel out.

In 1937 Lanteague received a lovely Bible from Mrs Jones (wife of the late Rev'd W.Jones) in memory of her husband.

1939 saw the special Jubilee services on the 6th, 7th and 11th June (*see Newspaper articles elsewhere in this book*). In April William Shanklin had become Treasurer and Deacon, Mrs Hannah Williams, Long Lane, was also a Deaconess, with Archibald Frazer John, Blaentidwell, being a Deacon.

31 July 1941 saw organist Lilian Shanklin marry James Callnon at Reynalton Chapel. A licence had been applied for at Lanteague Chapel but had not arrived in time.

In 1941 it states that the deeds are held by South Wales Congregational Trust from September and in the care of Mr J.M.H.Hawkins, Midland Bank, Bridgend. There was a solicitor's bill for perusing the Deeds and preparing the application to the Charity Commission for an order appointing the South Wales English Congregational Union (Incorporated) Trustees of the Chapel with Rev'd J.H.Phillips, B.G.Evans and William John and establishing a scheme for the future regulating of the charity. (*It was later stated in March 1979 that South Wales Congregational Trust held the deeds to the Chapel by order of the Charity Commission.*)

It was not until 4 January 1947 that the first wedding was held there – of John Callen and Constance Gladys Bradshaw. They received a gift of a Bible from the chapel.

In October 1948 Hugh James, Blackheath, was paid £15 12s 6d for painting the chapel in June and doing liming of the Vestry and roof repairs. In August 1949 he received £8 10s for more painting.

1949 saw the Diamond Jubilee celebrations of the building of the 'new' chapel.

In June 1955 they paid Miss Evans £2 10s for half a year's cleaning.

In August 1955 William and Margaret Shanklin and family gave a Communion Table. In September Hannah Williams and Mrs May Callen gave an aisle carpet. Carpet for the back of the pulpit was donated by

Mrs P.Phillips, Mr Glynne Phillips, Mrs Hannah Williams and Mrs S.Hodge.

In September 1955 the Secretary, Mr B.G.Evans, resigned through ill health. He had been a member for the past 50 years and was conferred with an honorary lifelong Deaconship of Lanteague Chapel for his long and faithful services. Mr Evans expressed a wish not to accept any gift for his long service. Mr W.Shanklin, Upper Castle Ely, then took over as Secretary and Mr Glynne Phillips, Brynhyfred, as Treasurer. On 25th Glynne Phillips and Wilfred Callen, Water Goch (*now The Hawthorns*), were appointed Deacons.

In October 1955 a wedding gift of a walnut coffee table was given to Rev'd and Mrs Stanley Jones from the Deacons and members.

In March 1956 pulpit clothes and table runners of blue velvet from an anonymous donor were dedicated.

The Manse at Longstone, Ludchurch, was used for the minister of Longstone and Lanteague – in April 1956 it was decided to give £25 towards its decoration.

In May 1956 Miss Bessie Evans resigned as cleaner and Mollie James took over at £5 a year.

A new pulpit chair was dedicated in May 1956, given by Mr B.G.Evans and his daughter Bessie.

On 14 April 1957 the agreement for the connection of electricity was signed – £7 10s for 6 years.

Also in 1957 Daniel Lewis of Penlan House, Tavernspite, bequeathed £25 to the chapel.

Hugh James was paid £8 for roof repairs in July 1957.

15 December 1957 saw the switching on of the electricity (by William Shanklin) and a dedication service. A fundraising concert was held in the Village Hall to fund the connection and £33 was raised.

Alfred Callen left a legacy of £50 to the chapel in September 1958.

Mr B.G.Evans died in 1958 and was buried in Templeton.

July 1959 saw the chapel receive £1 from Mr Dale of Tenby for the 'old organ'.

In November 1959 Hannah Williams, Katie Davies and Mr and Mrs Shanklin bought an organ from Dales in Tenby for £21 – it was dedicated on the 21st.

In 1960 Mollie James resigned as cleaner and was replaced by Miss Josephine Phillips. It was in this year that a Sunday school was started by Rev'd R.G.Cole.

For quite a few years around 1960 Mrs Bowen made the Anniversary cake.

The bad winter of 1963 also had its effects here. The December 1962 service on the 30th was cancelled because of snow and no service was again logged until 17 February 1963.

(The late Mike Evans stated, in his column in the Tenby Observer of 3 Feb 2003, that 'It started to snow at 3pm on Boxing Day (1962)....byroads remained impassable for weeks. In fact the road to Whitland from Llanteg and Tavernspite was closed until Good Friday'.)

The Bible was rebound in July 1963 for £3 18s.

In 1964 Lanteague Chapel reopened after being closed for two Sundays for renovation work, which had been carried out by Arthur Callen and Ronnie Glanville at a cost of £50.

Mrs Hannah Williams died on 29 June 1964. Mrs Williams had been a faithful member for more than 60 years and a Deacon for 30 years. She loved her chapel and would do all in her power to help at any time. She was loved by all that knew her and was greatly missed. Mrs Williams lived to 82 years and worshipped at Lanteague from her early years. Her husband died on 16 November 1953 and is buried in the same grave. She left £50 in her Will for the chapel.

Mr A.Callen was paid £16 10s 04d in June 1967 for repairs to the pulpit. And in July he received £48 for a concrete path in the chapel yard and repairs to the Vestry and toilet. The repairs consisted of:-

New piece of floor in the chapel where the stove was

New timber where stove pipes were

Concrete path down chapel yard

Repair crack above stable door

Hand rail on Vestry steps

Repair Vestry windows

Lime Vestry

Snowcem side of Vestry steps

Repair water troughs

Make coal house into toilet

New timber to support beams in stable and coal house

Lay pipes each side of chapel to carry rainwater from roof to each side of yard.

Also in December 1967 the chapel paid £26 to the Co-op at Kilgetty for eleven yards of carpet.

1969 - Mr J.O.Nicholls of Kilgetty was paid £104 13s 10d for reroofing and painting. He also removed the chimney.

1970 saw the death of Mrs Mary Phillips of Haulfryn, Red Roses, who was 78 years old. She had been a lifelong member and was always ready to help in any way until her illness of later years. She always attended every service and was sadly missed.

The Manse at Longstone was sold, with a third of the proceeds of £4,900 going to Lanteague (£1,558), with Longstone Chapel having two thirds. Longstone did not join the United Reform Movement so the partnership between the two chapels was now severed.

In 1972 Cissie Maud Williams, Whitland, left £10 to the chapel and an anonymous donor gave twelve communion glasses.

By the end of 1972 the cleaner had to give up through ill health after eleven years. In January 1973 Ruth Bevan was appointed cleaner. She received £10 a year, going up to £15 by 1974.

January 1973 - £10 donation received from the Will of Cissie Maud Williams.

In 1973 Lanteague joined the United Reformed Movement – 'we hope we have taken the right decision with God's guidance'.

December 1973 – Mr and Mrs Bertie John, Broadmoor, gave a hymn board in memory of Mr John's mother.

In 1974 the chapel must have decided to get tough with its wayward members. Two letters went out – one to Arthur Callen, Council House, to inform him that he was no longer a member of Lanteague Chapel as he had never attended services nor taken communion since 1958. The second letter went to Wilfred Callen of Long Lane, also informing him that he was no longer a member as he had not carried out the duties of Deacon since 1955 nor taken communion since 1964. They stated that 'the chapel has to be kept going by regular members attending, otherwise the chapel doors would have been closed years ago'.

(Note stating that this was the year of the 'great drought' – no rain for three months.)

1977 saw the purchase of a new organ – with a deposit of £36.84 in January, followed by the balance of £337.

In April 1977 the death is recorded of Mrs Margaret Gwendoline Shanklin of Cuckoo Wood, aged 93 years. She was the beloved wife of the Secretary Mr W.Shanklin and she was the eldest member of Lanteague Chapel and always attended regularly until her health failed her.

In September 1978 the Secretary, William Shanklin, retired, aged 88 years. He had given 43 years' service, first as Treasurer and then as Secretary. He was sadly missed. He had to retire due to failing health but still took an active interest and supported the chapel financially.

Deaconess and organist, Mrs Lilian Callnon, daughter of W.Shanklin, took over as Secretary from 17th September 1978.

Owing to extreme ill health, Mr Glynne Phillips, Haulfryn, was confined to hospital and forced to retire as Treasurer – he had served for 23 years.

In September 1977 Mr Cole was paid £40 for painting the chapel.

In 1978 cream and brown paint and putty was purchased for the outside - £18.32.

1978 also saw the drawing up of Burial Rules for the graveyard. These were copied down by Mrs Callnon for her father Mr Shanklin who was 88 years of age and according to Mrs Callnon was 'very shaky':-

Burials Committee to the officers of the church, who must be consulted before the burial in the burial ground adjacent to the chapel.

All members, their husbands and wives and their children will be given a free burial plot on their death, if the family wish to accept. For anyone else buried there, after consulting the committee, a charge will be made.

It was also decided, in view of keeping the yard tidy as far as possible, and also in line with other churches, in present-day rules, to allow traditional headstones, but not kerbs, owing to the difficulty of cutting grass between the graves. Headstones to be kept in line, as tidy as possible.

Photo: Carol Mason

Mrs Lillian Callnon, her father, Mr. William Shanklin (when he was presented with a Bible) and Mr. Roger Jones

From July 1978 William Shanklin was unable to attend services due to age, and was confined to home. He lived with his son Tom and daughter-in-law, but was still interested in chapel affairs. November 1978 saw two gifts purchased - William Shanklin received a Family Bible in recognition of 43 years service and Glynne Phillips received an inscribed wristwatch (presented at home on 19 December when he came out of hospital).

On 31 December 1978 the service was cancelled due to 'very heavy snow'.

In February 1980 a meeting was held to discuss the deeds. It was decided to continue Trusteeship with the Congregational Trust in co-ordination with the present Trustees of Lanteague Chapel – providing the charges are reasonable.

Trustees were Mrs Lilian Callnon, Mr William Shanklin (89 years) and Mr R.Jones.

(Mrs Callnon was Secretary, Mr Jones Treasurer and Mrs Jones Assistant Treasurer.)

The United Reformed Church Magazine covered the 'Tenby Group' – Amroth, Llanteg, Penally, St Florence and Tenby. In the May 1980 issue they said that for the Easter service they had welcomed Rev'd H.S.J.Gray, after his trip to Israel. 'It was good to see the oldest member, Mr W.Shanklin, who had been unwell and in bed all winter. He will be 90 in June. Eleri Jones was here on holiday from Wrexham – she is the daughter of our Treasurer and was given a Bible when she left to go teaching. We welcomed Andrew Mason, the 10-year-old son of Carol Mason and grandson of our Secretary, on holiday from Lingfield Hospital School, Surrey, and his health much improved. We were sorry to hear that Mr & Mrs Garrett were unwell, they usually regularly attend services.' Sympathies of the chapel also extended to Mrs Garrett on the death of her brother, Mr Tom Phillips. Miss Julie Hellings had returned from holiday abroad - good wishes to her mother for a return to good health.

In July 1980 the magazine recorded that they were sorry to hear of the death of Jack Garrett, husband of Millie Garrett of Middleton – 'we shall miss him from our worship and extend sympathy to Mrs Garrett in her great loss'. A Sankey Evening was held but there was a disappointing attendance with the chapel only being half full – however 'friendliness and warmth made up for it'. Again in December an evening of Sacred Films and Carols was held – very disappointing, very badly attended and the ladies had made mince pies and tea – 'rather a shame folks didn't turn up'. Through the winter Bible Study was held in members' homes – 'we enjoyed the fellowship'.

On 6 February 1981 Mr William Shanklin died suddenly at his home, Maindy, Pentlepoir. On many occasions there had been four generations of the family present at services. Mr Shanklin was 90 years old. During the funeral the chapel was full and people were out in the yard.

The March/April 1981 U.R.C. magazine had no Llanteg news submitted by Mrs Callnon owing to the death of her father, William Shanklin. The May/June magazine had a tribute by Mrs Callnon to her father which said:-

'A *deacon, member, past Secretary and Treasurer and to me a father for whom I thank God for his life and good example. He had been in fellowship at Llanteg for 46 years and before that at Penally U.R.C.*'.

A receipt was found relating to a new clock bought from Bisley Munt for £40 in August 1981. This clock was installed on the left wall and inscribed in memory of William Shanklin. A mower was also bought with money collected in his memory. The mower was to be kept at the home of Tom Shanklin as no suitable shed was available at the chapel and also it was Tom who mowed the yard.

The July/August 1981 U.R.C. magazine gave sympathy to Mrs Jones, The Downs, a regular worshipper, on the death of her brother-in-law. Mrs Carol Mason was unable to attend owing to ill health, also Andrew was unwell on the last two occasions he was home for half-term from Lingfield Hospital – he is now improving. They thanked their friends John Badham, David Shanklin and Mr Jenkins for helping members clean up and cut grass in the yard for the anniversary services.

The September/October 1981 magazine stated that they missed Mr and Mrs Deathridge from the services: Mr Deathridge was in hospital and they were 'remembered in our prayers'. Prayers were also said for young Andrew Mason who had had an accident on his bike and they were pleased to say he was progressing well. After the Royal Wedding celebrations in the village of sports, tea in the Hall, followed by an evening buffet and disco, the Mountain Chapel celebrated in song 'in our little chapel' on Sunday 2 August at 8pm. In November 1981 they wished Mrs Pincott happiness 'when she leaves next month'. Get well wishes were sent to the organist, Mrs Jackson, who had not enjoyed good health for the last few weeks.

Christmas 1981 saw the usual Carol Service – there was then very bad snow for weeks – 'most people almost locked in for 2 weeks, especially the farmers'.

At the start of 1982 services were cancelled until the end of January. There was bad weather and electricity cuts. The W.I. members delivered milk on sleighs around the village.

In June 1982 the chapel was only half-full for the Anniversary Service. Later in the year the members found it difficult to get preachers and sometimes took the services themselves. There were only seven members and sometimes only about ten at services – and less on many occasions. It was very disappointing, as no young people were present. As was so rightly foretold by Mrs Callnon – 'one fears for the future of the church'.

In 1983 the Secretary, Mrs Lilian Callnon, moved to Kilgetty, having sold the business (*Llanteg Garage*). It was decided to now only hold fortnightly services.

In 1984/5 a claim was made regarding structural damage to the porch – this was believed to have been caused by heavy lorries. The Welsh Office refuted this and said that although the porch was of good quality masonry and brickwork, it had been added after the chapel was built and therefore the walls were butted on rather than bonded in. They stated that it was evident there had been movement over the years as previous cracks had been repaired and that 'traffic does so as of right', and the problems stemmed from shallow foundations.

In 1985/6 Mr Cole had to repair the roof which was damaged in a storm. He was paid £600 as he also supplied materials and built a new gateway and installed a gate – the old gate was 'broken and posts finished' (*this was presumably the large gate by the Vestry*). It was necessary to protect the cemetery and graves and was 'a great improvement'. The front gate and entrance had been greatly improved about two years previously when the Welsh Office raised the Trunk Road and the entrance was altered. They built steps down inside the front gate from the road – 'it was very tidy'.

By 1986 fortnightly services would only consist of six or seven people. Deacons Mr Tom Shanklin and wife Megan did not attend services often due to his health and the distance to travel. Mrs Callnon, who herself was over 70 years old, found it difficult to travel from Kilgetty as she had no transport.

There was more storm damage in 1986 when £71 was spent on roof repairs.

In January 1987 members were shocked to hear of the death of Mr A.C.Hellings. Although not a member he would be missed, as he was always helpful, even helping in the pulpit, and they could always depend on him. It was quite a large funeral. Unfortunately there was a power cut during the service so there was no organ music, but the singing was good.

The 1987 Anniversary Service was poorly attended – Mrs Callnon was on the organ. The chapel was renovated both ends as the plaster had been falling off; the pulpit was also varnished. The shed was done up in the bottom of the yard. As there was no toilet now they put in an Elsan one 'for emergencies', until such time as they could put in a flush toilet 'when the membership increased'. Mr Treharne of Stepaside did the work for £725, with the toilet being given by Mrs Callnon. With the shed now able to be locked they kept the mower there – Mr P.Hellings had taken over keeping the yard mown – Mr T.Shanklin, who had heart trouble, was no longer able to do this and they were grateful to Mr Hellings for taking over. Mrs Callnon had kept the chapel clean and tidy for quite a few years but could no longer come from Kilgetty, so they were grateful to Mrs Jones (wife of the Treasurer), for taking on the cleaning and care of the chapel.

In 1988 they were down in funds as they always gave a lot to charity and again roof repairs cost £120, as did electrical repairs. They held the usual Carol Service but 'very small in numbers'.

1989 was the chapel's Centenary Year. The former minister, Rev'd T.J.Hopkins, was asked to the Anniversary Service (he had been at Lanteague from 1938-45 and was 78 years old but still taking three services on Sundays in the Pembroke area). The service was on May 28 at 2.30pm. The chapel was about full. Mr Brown of Tavernspite did the prayer and Mr David Shanklin of Pembroke Dock (former Sunday school pupil and later member) read the lesson. Mrs L.Callnon gave an address on the history of the chapel and Mr Peter Morgan of Manorbier closed in prayer. Mrs Brown was on the organ. Mrs Callnon had also arranged a concert with Kilgetty Male Voice Choir and Lady Artists (one lady was blind and she was presented with a donation for the Pembrokeshire Blind Fund). The concert was very good indeed with the chapel being nearly full and it was enjoyed by all present – friends from most local churches joined them for this occasion.

1990 was the 101st Anniversary – the service was held on May 27 with Rev'd Roy Parker from Camrose. There was a much smaller congregation than the previous year but the singing was good – 'like the atmosphere, and most friends of our church attended'.

In 1991 the Anniversary Service was on 26 May and the organist was Linda Shanklin – the daughter of David and Janet. This was Linda's first attempt to play at an event. There were about 25 present and Rev'd Frank Goodwin of Tenby presided.

Repairs were also needed in 1991 to the woodwork at each side of the chapel and loose slates were replaced – cracks in the chapel ceiling were also repaired. In December there was a small Carol Service of only five people – Mr Duffett presided. The Treasurer and his wife were ill and could not attend – but it was a nice service with Mrs Callnon on the organ.

A calender was published for 1993 (by Concept Photography, Swansea) with a lovely picture of the chapel on the front. The Anniversary Service was presided over by Rev'd Gillam of Haverfordwest with even fewer present. Mr Ron Hurlow played and his wife sang a solo.

There was an invoice from G.H.Evans of Kilgetty dated December 1994 for the sale of the following items:

14 foot pine table and 4 trestles, 2 matching bench seats - £30

Large pine scrub top kitchen table - £75

Victorian mahogany wind-out extending table - £190 (with turned legs, no spare leaf and a missing castor).

After commission etc. the chapel received £224.85 profit.

In 1995 the Anniversary Service was with Rev'd Hywel Brown and the attendance was much better than the previous year. Mr Ron Hurlow played the organ and Mrs Hellings recited a poem she had composed – which was very good.

In 1995 there was a total of four members and five coming to services – with no younger members.

Lanteague was known as Church No. 12E19 and in 1998 paid £84 for the upkeep of the yard. There was also £78 for the repairs to the organ. This was after they had paid £43 for organ repairs the previous year.

1996 started with only one service in January. Mrs Callnon wrote that the four or five members were all aged now and 'the Treasurer and his wife have poor health and are unable to attend'. With the severe winter so far most of them could not make it to the services. Also it was costly to heat the chapel and difficult to keep up financially – it was also getting difficult to get 'pulpit supplies' (ministers to take the services) now.

1997 started with no services in January – several people were not at all well so two services were cancelled. There were services in February but members were struggling to get there – not quite recovered – after this the fortnightly services resumed as usual. In April a message was received from friends at Zoar – they had closed their chapel the previous autumn because of floor problems. They had used to attend services and asked if, in the event of a death of a member, they could have the funeral at Lanteague. There was a meeting after the service on 13 April and it was agreed that the members of Lanteague were very willing for this to happen, but hoped that they would get help to clean and prepare the chapel if the occasion arose. Also in April the members discussed the future of the chapel: bearing in mind the age of the Officers and Trustees and the small membership, they felt it wise, if in the (hopefully) distant future, that Lanteague had to close, it was agreed that they wished any money in their funds to be used for the upkeep of the churchyard – in memory of all their past officers and members, who were, or would be, buried there – 'praying that this will not happen'. There was a funeral at the chapel in 1997 – Mrs Beatrice Davies. The service was held at Lanteague as Zoar Chapel had closed. Beattie, as she was known, had been Secretary of Zoar for many years and was a faithful member. The internment was at Zoar and it was a very large funeral.

In January 1998 the New Year Service was cancelled as the weather was very stormy. Also the Secretary Mrs Callnon had just come home from hospital after having had a big operation, so could not be present to play the organ (the organ was also giving quite a bit of trouble), other members were also ill. Twice monthly meetings continued in February. There was a poor attendance at both the Anniversary and Harvest Services.

1999 – the year began with lots of illnesses. The Treasurer and his wife had chest trouble and there was no service for several weeks. The Secretary was also unwell – she was in her 84th year. Mrs Callnon informed the Treasurer that she would be resigning at the end of the year - she was suffering from Parkinson's disease and getting worse; and she could not play the organ now, after 40 years, and also had failing sight. They struggled through the year with three members. Then there was sad news – Mrs Hellings had passed away. She was not a member 'but was very faithful and we miss her'. The Anniversary Service was held as usual, with poor attendance, preached by Rev'd Nanette Head of Tenby – she was very good.

A letter dated 25 October 1999 from the U.R.C. in Cardiff and copied to Nanette Head stated – 'It is important that the closing of the chapel is done with good order, both for the sake of yourselves as Officers and Church Members but also for the sake of the dignity of the way in which the church ends its history'.

Mrs Callnon wrote, 'I have told our few members previously of my intention and found it very difficult to keep attending and asked to meet them for a discussion. At our meeting in December 1999 (with moderator present) it was decided sadly that we would have to close the chapel – our last service would be the Carol Service on 19th December – but closing for service in January to enable us to dispose of the contents. The chapel officially closed on 30th January 2000. This was decided after we were informed by U.R.C. that they meant to sell it for a dwelling, and as they held the deeds they were the legal owners of the property'.

In January 2000 Mrs Callnon received a letter from U.R.C. Wales. They stated that they consented to her request to allow the three remaining members of the chapel to be buried in the graveyard after the chapel closed. The Trust officers were 'happy to accede to your request'. They also stated that the Trust would also give 'consideration' to the future maintenance of the graveyard. They had arranged to meet a surveyor at the chapel on the 13th to discuss the future of the chapel site.

In March 2000 a letter was again received from the U.R.C. to thank Mrs Callnon (former Secretary) and Mr Jones (former Treasurer) for the cheque for £2795.10 which was the closing balances of the three bank accounts in the name of Lanteague U.R.C.

Also in January 2000 Rev'd Dr K.Littler (of Pendine, Marros and Eglwys Cummin) wrote to Mrs Callnon to thank her for giving the organ (from Lanteague Chapel) to Marros. It had been transported to St Lawrence for the funeral of John Howells. The only organ they had had before was so bad no one would play it. "Giving your lovely organ from the Chapel, Mr Bryant Rees was able to play it for us at the funeral and this made a great difference to the proceedings. I am most distressed that it was necessary to close the chapel. We will think of you every time we have a service and will certainly remember you in our prayers." They had been doing renovation work and Rev'd Littler said, "a flag flies from the tower for the first time in many, many years and the congregation has grown very noticeably".

In March 2000 the U.R.C. in Cardiff wrote to Paul Lucas & Son instructing them to apply for outline planning permission to convert the building for residential use prior to advertising the property for sale. He was hopeful that this could be obtained and the site sold fairly quickly.

On 8 March 2000 Barclays Bank wrote to the Treasurer and Secretary informing them that they had forwarded all the money in the three accounts to the U.R.C. in Cardiff i.e. - £72.05, £1226.84 and £1496.21 – a total of £2795.10. The Chapel had even paid the insurance up to December 2000.

These chapel records will eventually be deposited in Haverforwest Record Office should anyone wish to consult them.

After local campaigning the chapel was saved from being converted into a dwelling but was partially demolished and handed over to Amroth Community Council to become a Garden of Remembrance for the village. With the help of a grant from PLANED, fundraising and donations from relatives, the area was gravelled and planters installed. The Vestry was sold by the U.R.C. and divided off from the graveyard to become a dwelling - Katelios. The U.R.C. donated funds to enable an Information Board to be erected detailing the history of the chapel.

MOUNTAIN CHAPEL – CAMBRIA ARCHAEOLOGY SURVEY – 2002/3
by Ruth Roberts

This survey by Cambria Archaeology was commissioned by Paul Williams, the developer of the chapel site, and was part of the archaeological condition placed on planning consent (*this was kindly donated to the History Society when Mr Williams sold Katelios and moved away*). The proposed development of the site involved the partial demolition of the chapel leaving the base walls standing to a height of about a metre and leaving it as part of a garden feature.

To the rear a new house was to be built beyond the graveyard and adjacent to the small vestry.

The report describes the chapel as rectangular with an arched double front door. The vestry was also rectangular with three entances on the ground floor and a brick chimneystack. Part of the ground floor was of rough cobbles, divided into two with bays with a tongue and groove partition and would have been used as a stable. This partition contained graffiti on its south side, which, although difficult to read, read as:-

H Glanvel? (*Glanville*)
W Morse?
Margo...play mor?
J R Lewis

N G Lewis
Owan Jones

Frank James
Full time Rabbit Trapper

John Lewis
Owen Jones
Oct 7th 1947
Very wet

Very wet day July 3 1932

April 21st 1936

The entrance on the western side was of double width (possibly for a cart) giving access to the northern ground floor. This had been partially blocked by a wall and had recently contained a chemical toilet and had a cement floor.

The northern entrance gave access to a flight of stone stairs leading to the first floor. The top of the stairs was boxed in with panelling. In the northern wall were the remains of a small range.

The new building has retained the structure of the vestry.

Report 2003/19 Project 45433 Cambria Archaeology.

1904 SALES NOTICE (CRUNWERE FARM AND RIGMANHILL)
by Ruth Roberts

Contained in a Sales Notice dated 14 April 1904 is the sale, among other properties, of Crunwere and Rigman Hill Farms.

Crunwere Farm – 'Comprising 87 acres 2 roods or thereabouts of rich pasture and arable land and now in the occupation of Messrs Williams as yearly tenants.'

Rigmans Hill - '......and closes of land called 'Rhydgoch*', situate adjoining lot IV (Crunwere Farm) in the said parish of Crunwere, containing altogether 33 acres, 2 roods or thereabouts of rich pasture and arable land and in the same occupation as the last mentioned lot. With this lot will be included all that small burgage or piece of land situate adjoining and comprising 1 rood, 30 poles or thereabouts called 'Shipping Hill', which is held for the residue of a term of 999 years at a peppercorn rent.'

(Lots IV and V are let to Messrs Williams at an entire rent of £115 10s and will first be offered in one lot and if not so sold, then in the two lots as above.)

Rhydgoch is believed to have been on the eastern side of the road at the bottom of the hill opposite Broomylake entrance, on the road from Llanteg to Tavernspite.

De Rutzen Hotel Sales Notice 1904.

LLANTEGLOS HOUSE SALE 1903 AND 1940
by Ruth Roberts

Two sales notices give details of Llanteglos:

26 March 1903 – For Sale by auction at the De Rutzen Arms Hotel, Narberth a 'genteel country residence with about 22 acres, lately occupied by Mrs Purser, deceased'.

The house is in well shrubbed grounds and has an entrance hall, dining and drawing rooms, 4 large bedrooms and store room, large kitchen, pantry, scullery, cellar and dairy. There is also a two stalled stable, coach and cart houses and other conveniences. A large kitchen garden and well stocked orchard. There is plenty of fox hunting, shooting and fishing in the neighbourhood.

1 June 1940 - Llanteglos and 22½ acres were up for auction at The Royal Playhouse, Tenby, and were offered in three lots:

Lot 1 – Llanteglos and just over 10½ acres. The house was described as being built of stone and Caernarfon slated and consisted of entrance hall, drawing room, dining room, kitchen, sculleries, 2 pantries, box room or maids bedroom, W.C., wooden back porch, 4 large bedrooms, bathroom (H&C), W.C. and airing cupboard.

The house is approached by a short drive through the grounds which are attractively laid out. Electric light is fitted to the house, cottage and outbuildings. Hot and cold water is laid throughout the house. The public water supply has been brought in and in addition a pump on the premises also gives a good supply of water.

The back drive of the residence leads past a cottage which is stone built and Caernarfon slated and consists of 2 parlours, kitchen, 2 bedrooms and greenhouse.

Alongside is a stone built and corrugated roofed small garage and a large garage or workroom. *(Later to become The Wanderer's Rest.)*

In the garden is a stone built and Caernarfon slated engine house, from which is worked the electric light for the premises by means of a

'Petter' engine, the accumulator room lying over it.

Hitherto the property was established as a poultry farm, but is now partly dismantled.

Two main poultry sheds (practically new), and a number of arcs and material are also available for purchase, if desired.

The premises, with pasture land to the front, form the complete lot.

Lot 2 – Two fields situated on the opposite side of the road and lying on each side of York Place (*now York House*) having a frontage to the road leading from Llanteglos to Llanteg (2.24 acres).

Lot 3 – Two fields near Lot 2 on the south side of the crossroads on the lane leading down to Ledgerland (9.59 acres).

THE SOUTH PEMBROKESHIRE DIALECT IN THE LLANTEG LOCALITY
by Noel H.Davies

Since leaving Bryneli Farm for London in 1943 to enter the wide wide world of work, I have often mused over the distinctive and well recognisable South Pembrokeshire dialect as spoken in and around Llanteg in the first half of the twentieth century.

The interpretation of the origin of words is best left to specialists in the field – a field I would not dare to enter!

However, I feel it would be a pity if the old words were lost to posterity and it is pleasing that much work has been done over the years to catalogue them.

As an interested layman, I have 'dipped my toe in the water' by perusing the following publications:-

Guide to Place Names and Dialects of Pembrokeshire by P.Valentine Harris (H.G.Walters (Publishers) Ltd, 1974)

The English Dialect of South Pembrokeshire by B.G.Charles (Pembrokeshire Record Society 1982)

English in Wales: Diversity, Conflict and Change, edited by Nikolas Coupland in association with Alan R.Thomas (1990 - Multilingual Matters Ltd, Bank House, 8a Hill Road, Clevedon, Avon, BS21 7HH) – Chapter II – The Conservative English Dialects of South Pembrokeshire by David Parry is of particular interest. It examines variations of the dialect and is based on data collected between 1969 and 1975 for six localities south of the Pembrokeshire Landsker – Camrose, Wiston, Marloes, Llangwm, Angle and St Florence.

Some of the words appearing in the above publications (and, with the sole exception of grub, *not* appearing in my Oxford Concise Dictionary) which stick in my mind from the 1930s and 40s are:-

Aclush – all to pieces, to a mess, a mix-up

Bauk, Bork – to belch

Belge – to bellow

Bickning, Bigning – a beacon, a summit of a hill (as in Bigning Farm, near Pendine)

Branders – a tripod or trivet for supporting a pot or kettle over a fire on the ground

Brimsy – on heat (for sows)

Caffle – to entangle, to confuse, to bewilder

Chimblin – chilblain

Coppice – the flap of a countryman's trousers

Crut – a boy, lad

Culf – a hunk of bread

Danted – daunted, discouraged

Doybil – a pickaxe, a combination of mattock and hatchet

Disle, Dissel, Deistle, Distel – a thistle

Drang – a narrow passage between walls or hedges (as a pupil of the County School and in digs at 10 St James St, Narberth, I kicked many a ball back and fore in the drang off that street)

Emmak – the ant

Grain – cleanliness

Grouts – the dregs of tea or coffee

Grubber – an eater, feeder ('he's a good grubber' to describe a man with a hearty appetite)

Hobbel – a small load of hay

Jonnack – fair, honest, straightforward, satisfactory, agreeable

Kift – clumsy, awkward

Lab – to gossip, to blab, let out secrets

Lonker – shackle with which animals were hobbled

Miskin – a dunghill, manure heap

Mitch – to play truant

Moil – to root in the ground like a pig

Pile – to throw (e.g. stones)

Rammas – a long tedious story

Scadly – greedy

Skew – a settle (Welsh *ysgiw*)

Swaf – to spread swathes of hay abroad

Tamping – exceedingly annoyed (as in 'he was tamping mad')

Tare – brazen faced (I well remember my mother describing a crow getting too near for comfort 'that old crow is very tare')

Tump – a heap of hay ready for carting, a hay-cock.

I wonder how many of these old words are heard in the area nowadays? The Society would be pleased to hear from readers with comments on the above list, along with any additions they may have.

The British Library Sound Archive is an excellent source for those wishing to delve deeper into English as spoken by people in Wales and there is much information on their website. The Wales entry (2008) is based on hundreds of recordings made by David Parry and Robert Penhallurick of Swansea University over the last forty years and includes conversations recorded in Pembrokeshire at Marloes and Newport.

Also a new book, *Below the Landsker*, has just been published by Rob Scourfield and Keith Johnson (Jackydando Books) which is a dictionary of South Pembrokeshire dialects.

EXTRACTS FROM CRUNWERE RELATED NEWSPAPER ARTICLES
annotated by Ruth Roberts
Sunday Traffic

'The Sunday motor traffic on the main road passing through Llanteague is enormously increasing, and several motorists drive recklessly and furiously, it is highly dangerous for little children to be on the road by themselves' (*they ought to see it now – 86 years later!*)

Narberth Weekly News 28 June 1923.

Crunwere Man Captains Indian Hockey Team – 1923

'The hockey team of the A Company 2/16th Punjab Regiment won the Inter-Company Hockey Cup for 1922/23. The team, captained by Captain Noel James Glanville Jones (with the exception of Captain Jones) was made up entirely of native players.

Captain Jones is the son of Mr Benjamin Jones and the late Mrs Jones of Heatherland, Llanteg, and has spent three years in India. Captain Jones is well known in Narberth and his father is a popular member of the Narberth Board of Guardians.'

Narberth Weekly News 15 November 1923.

Reverend Dalton, Rector of Crunwere
(Robert Davies – 1924)

'In a letter written by Robert Davies of Swansea he states that when he was a small boy his grandfather used to relate to him some experiences that he had had with Mr Dalton (the parson), whom he lived with as a servant. His wage was next to nothing and his food was coarse – barley bread with a slice of white bread once at Christmas time, and at times they would have to go to Trenewydd Farm for fresh supplies as part of the tithe. I am not blaming the parson, but such were the prevailing conditions of that time just over 100 years ago (*in 1820s*).'

Narberth Weekly News 7 February 1924.

Roads – Ancient and Modern
(Ben Price 1924)

Mr Ben Price writes of the old road from Lanteague to Tavernspite which he believed was possibly thousands of years old, based on the fact that in places the surface of the road is considerably below the level of the adjoining fields, probably as a result of long use.

Mr Price goes on to state that old British roads, apart from those built by the Romans, were probably, at first, just tracks for pack animals. They would have been gradually adopted for wheeled traffic with no foundations or the easing of gradients. The earth was soon washed away by the little stream which followed the depression formed by the traffic, and the rock was soon exposed. This was mostly as in the case we are considering, of a soft, shaley, crumbly nature near the surface, and the traffic, greatly assisted by the water, gradually wore this down with the water carrying the loose materials away. A good road was an unknown thing little more than a century ago, particularly by-roads.

Narberth Weekly News 14 February 1924.

Recollections of Robert Davies – 1924

In the Narberth Weekly News Mr Robert Davies of Swansea is replying to correspondence by Mr Ben Price. He states that he is no relation to the family at Bevelin (*sic*) although he knew them well. Mr Davies states that he is the eldest son of Billy and Nanny, The Palace, the names by which they were best known. 'It is no fault of mine that I was born poor, and the eldest son of a large family. I had to commence young, with but little education, to carve my way through life's rugged path, and during the sixty years on this planet I have at least learnt a little and I know that many a good heart beats beneath a ragged coat.'

Mr Davies goes on to speak of Mr T.Morris, Morfabuchan, who had been dead for over 30 years. He was a self-taught sculptor of no mean renown who is believed to have had something to do with the Prince Albert Monument in Tenby (with some of the stones coming from Pullh quarry). He was also a rough country poet, and would always keep you 'on the laugh' with some of his ditties. He was also a singer and fond of his fiddle.

'For myself, I can only relate one experience, which was during the time he was erecting a tombstone in Amroth churchyard. It was a beautiful moonlight night and I was homeward bound, as a boy, from Amroth Castle, when Mr Morris was entertaining the old folks. I think the old lady's name was Beattie Thomas. Nothing remains of the old haunt now, but it was close to Billy and Mary Isaac, and Thomas and Mary Evans, the Wood Cottages. It has left me something to remember, but alas all the old faces have passed over.'

Narberth Weekly News 21 February 1924.

Dick a' Telpin
(Ben Price 1925)

Ben Price recalls that he also knew 'Dick a' Telpin', when he lived in the little farm overlooking delightful little Telpin Bay. 'About 25 years ago I visited Amroth with some of my family, we happened to have our tea in the cottage on the side of the hill beyond New Inn, and in the course of conversation with the good lady of the house I found that she was, unless my memory fails me, Dick a' Telpin's widow. From the other side of the road to this house there was, and is I think, a path leading to the Black Rock. There is a well of good water on the way down.'

Narberth Weekly News 10 September 1925.

Local Will – Mr J.C.S.Glanvile, Crunwere – 1927

'Mr James Cox Slade Glanville, of Llanteg, Crunwere, farmer, who died on January 22nd 1926, left estate of the gross value of £7,398, with next personality of £670. Probate of the Will dated December 1st 1923 has been granted to Mr George Joseph Collins of Kilgetty. Mr Glanville left his estate in trust for his wife and his daughter Winifred Irene during their lives, with the remainder to his sons Wilfred David Glanville,

Harcourt Reginald Glanville, James Yorke Glanville and William Leslie Glanville. His sons Wilfred and Harcourt to get one half the amounts that the other sons do.'

Narberth Weekly News 2 June 1927.

Captain Jones's Meeting with a Tiger – 1927
Death of the Great Cattle Destroyer

Whilst many may object to the death of this beautiful beast we must remember that people's outlooks were completely different over 80 years ago and also this animal had been destroying villagers' cattle – it was not simply a 'trophy kill'.

The following extracts are from an interesting letter dated 30 June 1927 received by Mr Benjamin Jones of Heatherland, Llanteg, from his son Mr Noel Jones who is an Officer in the 2nd Battalion, 16th Punjab Regiment, Sanger, India.

'On Thursday 23rd I realised my ambition and killed a tiger measuring 8 feet 8 inches – not a very big one but a great heavy animal that five of us couldn't move! This is roughly how it happened. Tigers do a lot of damage amongst the villagers; this one had already taken a large toll. Its procedure when killing never varies much. A cautious and silent approach to within twenty yards of its victim, a rush and spring, fangs buried deep into the throat and a backward wrench – the animal is dead with a broken neck. The tiger then drags its kill to some quiet spot and feeds, starting from the hindquarters. Having fed it goes off for a drink of water and will then lie up for the rest of the day. In the evening or night it will re-appear and continue its meal.

When on the prowl for food it moves by well defined tracks and water courses. In order to get in touch with our tiger the plan was roughly this:

First we searched around all water for marks – this localised the animal. We searched for tracks leading to it, and tied up a young buffalo on the most likely approach. The next day going down early in the morning there was no buffalo. The rope that had tethered him (¾ inch doubled), had been snapped like cotton and blood was on the ground with a distinct path into the jungle. Tiger's work – he had killed and dragged – so far so good. We followed the drag cautiously as it was quite possible that the tiger would still be on its kill. I had two native shikaris (native hunters) with me, both unarmed, but expert trackers and full of courage. I had a heavy double barrelled high velocity rifle loaded and cocked ready for immediate action. On we went. A splash of blood here and broken grass there gave the line. About four hundred yards took us to the top of a hill. Suddenly the shikari whispered "there he is"! The kill was lying under a tree. The tiger had left it either to go to water or possibly to lie up for the day. A quiet conference – the animal must be killed when he returned. Nearby was a leafy teak tree. We decided to tie up a 'machan' in it, and I would sit up for the tiger. A 'machan' is a sort of concealed platform constructed generally of a native string bed and the branches of trees. Whilst preparations for its construction were going forward I returned to camp – some six miles away – to get ready for the evening. This meant bringing out food, drink, blankets, skinning knives, flashlight, etc., for a possible night in the jungle. I was back at 3pm and climbing up the tree took up my position in the machan. The kill was dragged out. I came to the aim and showed them the exact spot where I wanted it. Everything ready, the kill was anchored by a short rope to the stump of a tree. The shikaris cleared off, and I was alone in the jungle awaiting the return of the tiger. Three hours passed; the jungle was silent except for the occasional cries of the peacock and sometimes a cuckoo. At 6 o'clock I suddenly heard a herd of deer in the distance give their alarm – a short and quickly repeated 'whoa – whoa – whoa'!! I knew at once that the tiger was on the move, and kept my eyes glued to a small peephole I had made in the screen of leaves surrounding my head. 6.30pm came, but no tiger. I began to think that the deer had given a false alarm or had probably been disturbed by some wandering villager. I was hungry and I had with me a tin of sardines and two chipatties. These I proceeded to eat, and then began to feel sleepy. The jungle was as silent as the grave. A gently breeze nestled through the leaves, a few mosquitoes buzzed, the sun going down behind a bank of cloud, and night was coming. It was a peaceful scene. I got drowsier! Then I thought I would have another look out. Imagine my surprise, for there standing right underneath my tree, turning his magnificent head slowly from side to side, was an enormous tiger – a wonderful picture of strength and grace. No wonder, I thought, the whole jungle gave way to him. He turned, and without a sound went up to the kill soft footed and as silent as a cat. I expected him to start feeding and whilst thus engaged I meant to take a shot between the withers. However he did not do as I anticipated and instead got his great teeth into the hind quarters of the dead buffalo and pulled and pulled. At any second the rope might have snapped. I grabbed my rifle and pushed it over the top of the machan, cocking it as I did so. I aimed between the eyes and fired. The tiger dropped the kill and jumped up with a tremendous angry roar. I fired again. Down he went with a crash, shoulder covered in blood, but still roaring defiance. He struggled half up and I gave him another in the shoulder. His head went down immediately and he began to give a sort of choking gasping growl. Another shot into the shoulder and silence. I looked at him through my binoculars, watching for any movement. An ear twitched – that was enough – he got another one. A tiger will fight till he is dead. I waited five minutes – no further movement. I climbed down my tree, whistled up the shikaris and examined the dead tiger – took photographs, measured him, and started work to remove the skin. Working by the light of an ordinary hurricane lantern, and with an old bayonet and a pocket knife, it took us an hour.

Many villagers arrived and the rejoicing on the way home at the death of the great destroyer of cattle was great.'

Narberth Weekly News 18 August 1927.

Summer Soccer – 1928

'Local football teams, as was the case last year, are being formed in and around Red Roses, and every evening the local lads vie with each other in chasing a ball about after a hard day's trudge behind the plough or harrows. The hotter the evening the more they appear to enjoy it. Eglwys Cummin has already met Llanteague in deadly combat, and some wonderful displays have been witnessed. There is no talk of cricket to be heard anywhere. No doubt it is far too slow a game.'

Narberth Weekly News 17 May 1928.

Motor Cycle Accident – 1928

'Whilst on her way to Whitland on Wednesday last week Mrs Davies, Milton, Llanteague, who was riding pillion behind her son, Mr Robert Davies, on his motorcycle, fell heavily to the ground and received extensive injuries. She was conveyed to her home, having been rendered unconscious, and was found to be suffering from concussion. It will be some weeks before she is able to leave her bed.'

Narberth Weekly News 17 May 1928.

Lanteague Cross Accident – 1928

'A serious accident was narrowly averted on Monday at Lanteague Cross.

111

It appears that about 11.30am the Rev'd R.Jackett was proceeding down Rectory Hill in his car and, driving slowly on approaching the cross-roads, sounded his horn. Not hearing the sound of another horn or aware that a vehicle was approaching, he proceeded to cross the road, when a car suddenly appeared. The driver of the latter could see that there was not room to pass and turned his car quickly right into the hedge. Had this car gone another few inches it would have been upset into a deep ditch. At the spot where the accident occurred there is a blind corner and several accidents have been narrowly averted. It is also a danger to the schoolchildren and steps should be taken before a fatal accident occurs.'

(The crossroads has changed considerably over the years – being raised and straightened to remove the blind corner. Imagine trying to drive out onto the main road without stopping today?)

Narberth Weekly News 8 November 1928.

Road Improvements - 1930

'It is of interest to learn that the County Council intend carrying out improvements at the dangerous corner known as Llanteague Cross. The necessary material has arrived and undoubtedly the work will be carried out in the near future. Several accidents have occurred at this spot and it will be welcome news to all road users that the corner is to be rendered less dangerous.'

Narberth Weekly News 23 January 1930.

Car Accident – Crunwere Motorist Involved – 1930

'A serious accident was narrowly averted on Friday last when two powerful cars collided on the Commercial crossroads, Narberth. It appears that about 6pm, Mr W.B.Davies, County Councillor, Trenewydd Farm, Crunwere, was driving his Alvis car along the Station Road towards the town, and was about to proceed towards Spring Gardens when a Humber car, driven by Mr Gwyn Nicholas Jones, London, appeared from Jesse Road, going in the direction of St James Street. A collision was inevitable, but with great presence of mind Mr Davies quickly turned his car to the left and so avoided a serious accident.

Mr Wolff, schoolmaster, Crunwere, was with Mr Davies in the car, and the driver of the Humber had his father and two ladies with him. Fortunately no one was injured. Both cars were badly damaged, the Alvis having a mudguard smashed, front axle bent and the main chassis damaged. The steering gear of the Humber was broken and one wheel and mudguard damaged. It is understood that the Alvis was insured.

Many accidents have occurred on the commercial crossroads and the one on Friday should again serve to emphasise the pressing need of an improvement at this dangerous stop.'

Front Page, Narberth, Whitland & Clynderwen Weekly News
2 October 1930.

Crunwere Hall Packed Out – People Faint
Girls' Friendly Society – A Fine Performance – 1932

'Crunwere Schoolroom (*then the only hall in the village – now a dwelling called Seabreeze*) was packed to its utmost capacity on Saturday last at 7 o'clock, half an hour before the Girls' Friendly Society concert was due to commence.

The Girls' Friendly Society formed a 'Gypsy Troup', which proved a brilliant success last year. The accommodation was too small and many people failed to gain admission. During the performance several persons fainted in the rear of the school; there being only seating room for half. Surely the time is ripe for the parishioners to get together and build a suitable hall for such events. (*It would be another 16 years before Llanteg did eventually have its own Public Hall.*)

Great credit is due to Mrs Grismond Williams, Llanteglos, who was responsible for the concert and all the girls who worked in harmony to make it a huge success. Miss R.Griffiths, who was responsible for the dresses, had worked tirelessly, and Mr Hawes, Heatherland, who at the last minute had acted as accompanist due to the illness of Miss Katie Thomas.

Those taking part were Misses M.Morris, H.John, M.Phillips, C.Hodge, M.Oriel, H.Davies, B.Davies, B.Morris, M.Morris, P.Morris, E.Hodge, G.Phillips, H.Hodge, L.Davies, P.Davies, K.Morris, and F.Phillips. All artists played their parts splendidly.'

Narberth Weekly News 28 January 1932.

Crunwere's Place in the Centuries
Mr Charles F.Shepherd's new book on Crunwere – 1933

'The "Weekly News" has been favoured with an advance copy of a new historical survey of St Elidyr, Crunwere, published by Mr Charles F.Shepherd A.L.A., now living at The Downs, Wenvoe, near Cardiff.

The booklet is undoubtedly one of the most valuable contributions that has yet been made to the permanent records of the history of the district. Mr Shepherd deals extensively with the ancient parish church and he throws illuminating side-lights on the derivation of many quaint place names in the Narberth district.

He has obviously devoted great care in conducting his research, for he refers to all the existing historical records relating to the parish.

The booklet, which contains a photograph of the Parish Church (taken by the author), is one of absorbing interest, and should enjoy a wide circulation throughout the county. It is priced at 6d.

The author, who has already published a similar work entitled "A Short History of St George-super-Ely", dedicates his new work "To my mother-in-law" and in the brief preface he writes, "I have to thank Mrs E.J.Jones, Oakland, Templeton, whose generosity has made its publication possible".

At its conclusion Mr Shepherd writes, "This account of Crunwere parish is of necessity brief, but it shows that the parish is one of great age. Through it cannot boast of a ruined castle or any antiquarian remains such as cromlechs etc., yet the old church still stands as a witness as it did in days gone by. Round it are centred memories that will be forever green, and here will worship the descendants of those who, too, have followed in their fathers' footsteps".'

Narberth Weekly News 28 September 1933.

Mr Charles Shepherd,
January 1992

Photo: Betty James

Llanteg History Society is indebted to Mr Shepherd's publication which formed the starting point for our continual researches into Crunwere Parish. I am sure Mr Shepherd would be saddened to realise that the 'descendants' he spoke of would now no longer be allowed into the church which he appreciated so much, as it has been closed for services since 2006 as it was unsafe. It was finally made redundant in 2009 with a final open-air service being held on August 2nd.

114

Concert Postponed – 1937

'The Influenza epidemic has begun to rage in the village. In some cases whole families have been stricken down whilst three-fourths of the schoolchildren are already affected. The Llanteg Concert Party has likewise not escaped, and so many of its members are "hors de combat", that the concert, which was to have been given by them tomorrow (Friday) under the leadership of the Rector (Rev'd D.Morgan), himself a victim of the epidemic, has had to be postponed until Easter. It is to be earnestly hoped that all sufferers will experience a speedy and complete recovery.'

Narberth Weekly News 4 February 1937.

Llanteg Man's Bride – 1937
Pretty Wedding at Eglwys Cymmin Church

'A wedding of considerable local interest was solemnised on Wednesday of last week between Mr Brinley Davies, son of the late Mr James Davies and Mrs Davies, Coombs Head, Llanteg, and Miss H.Hulin A.L.C.M., daughter of Mr and Mrs A.Hulin, Castle Lloyd Farm, Pendine.

The bride was charmingly gowned in white satin and wore a veil with orange blossoms. Her bouquet was of Madonna lilies. The bridesmaids were Miss Gwyneth James and Miss Beatrice Davies, Mrs Rex Evans was Matron of Honour and the flower girls were Mavis Griffiths (niece of the bridegroom), and Jane Wilson (niece of the bride). The best man was Mr Leslie Davies (brother of the bridegroom) and the groomsmen were Messrs Norman Jenkins and Rex Evans.

The gift of the bride to the groom was a pair of gold cufflinks, while the groom's gift to the bride was a fox fur. The bridesmaids received gifts of necklaces of gold chain and pearls, and the flower girls were given gold bracelets. A reception was held at Dolwar Café, Guildhall Square, Carmarthen, with between 70 and 80 guests. The honeymoon is being spent touring the Midlands and the bride's going away outfit was a grey tailored costume with hat and shoes to tone. Mr and Mrs Davies, who will make their home in Whitland, were the recipients of many costly presents.'

Narberth Weekly News 19 August 1937.

Sports Winners - 1937

'Hearty congratulations to the following upon their excellent performances at the Jeffreyston and District Coronation Charity Sports. Mr Robert (*Bob*) Davies was winner of the first prize in the one mile open handicap cycle race, and also winner of the Silver Cup and first prize in the two mile open handicap cycle race. In the one mile novice cycle race Trevor Wolff won first prize and James Glanville third prize (confined to Pembrokeshire). May further success attend the efforts of these three Llanteg boys in the future.'

Narberth Weekly News 26 August 1937.

Consecration of Crunwere Churchyard – 1937

'On Tuesday last the Bishop of St Davids consecrated the new churchyard at Crunwere Church. Before the service began every available seat was filled, and after prayers the Rector of Crunwere, Reverend D.Morgan, headed a procession followed by the Lord Bishop, attended by his Chaplain, the two Crunwere Churchwardens, the clergy in their robes, the Sunday School and a large number of parishioners and people from outlying districts who all walked around the new burial ground.

A halt was made while the Bishop performed the sacred rite of consecration. A service followed in the church. At the close of the service all proceeded to the school, where an excellent tea was served by Mrs Morgan, wife of the Rector, assisted by several members of the local branch of the Mothers' Union.

Everyone felt deeply grateful for the glorious weather which helped to ensure the success of the event, which was probably unique in the annals of Crunwere Parish.'

Narberth Weekly News 14 October 1937.

Lanteague Church's Jubilee (Mountain Chapel) – 1939

'The Jubilee of Lanteague Congregational Church was celebrated last Tuesday afternoon when the 50 years of the present chapel and the history of the cause at Llanteg were reviewed by a former pastor who ministered there for 23 years.

The attendance was not very large at the afternoon service, mainly due to the commencement of the hay making season.

The Rev J.H.Phillips gave a very interesting history of the Church which was as follows:

"The first Chapel was erected a short distance from the present building in 1820 by the parishioners for a schoolroom. It was afterwards used as a Chapel and had sitting accommodation for 40 people. The worshippers paid 1s a year rent. In the year 1864 a Congregational Church was formed and the first Communion was held the Rev'd

116

J.Davies, Carvan, and Joshua Lewis, Henllan, being the officiating ministers. Many years ago I was told by some of the older parishioners that wonderful meetings were held in the old chapel, meetings of great religious fervour and also that many souls were won to Jesus Christ. With the passing of time the old Chapel became dilapidated and it was necessary that a new and larger building should be erected. In 1889 during the ministry of the Rev Lewis James the present Chapel, which has a sitting accommodation for 150 people, was built. It cost £170 and was opened on 4th December free of debt. The ministers who officiated at the opening services were: Rev J.E.Griffiths, Pembroke Dock; D.M.Picton, Templeton; W.Morgan, Saundersfoot; J.Williams, Carvan; and Lewis James, Brynbank. Large congregations attended and inspiring services were held. At that time Mr Tom Phillips, Longland (*Longlane*); Mr Ben Lewis, Tavernspite; Mr William Lewis, New House; Mr William Callen, Goitre, Mr David Williams, Trenewydd, and several noble women were staunch supporters of the cause. In 1900 an organ was introduced and the singing then greatly improved. Mr William Jenkins, Lanteague, and Mr Ben Lewis, Tavernspite, acted for years as presenters.

The First Pastor

The first minister of Lanteague was the Rev. J.Davies, Carvan, and he was followed in rotation by Revs D.Mathias, Saundersfoot, Heber Williams, Templeton, Lewis James, Brynbank, J.Howell Phillips, Tiers Cross, William Jones and T.J.Hopkins.

I received on July 4th 1902 a call to the pastorate of the United Congregational Churches of Longstone, Amroth and Lanteague. I was offered a salary of £60. The call was signed by the deacons of the three churches, those who signed for Lanteague were David Williams and Benjamin Evans. The deacons of one of the churches asked me if I was a T.A. (*total abstainer?*), fortunately, I was; I afterwards discovered that not one of them was at the time.

When I came here the Church had a membership of 24. The average attendance at the Sunday School was 17. When I left there was a bigger membership and more attended the Sunday School. In 1904 a new porch was built and those who worship here in the winter months know its value. That year too the late Mr Davies, Oaklands, gave £50 to build a vestry and when the money was afterwards taken from the bank there was £3 15s interest. In 1907, the vestry, which cost £64 15s, was built. Free haulage was made and the extra £11 (*needed to pay for the vestry*) came from the proceeds of a concert. It was built by Mr Dan Williams,

Carvan, who had previously built the chapel. The vestry with the stable underneath has been a great asset to the church. During Chapel renovations religious services have been held there. The scroll behind the pulpit was paid for by Mrs Richards, Post Office, Amroth, and her son Thomas Daniel Richards.

On March 24th 1945 new trustees were appointed as follows: J.Howell Phillips, the Retreat; T.D.Richards, Post Office; B.G.Evans, Pendeilo Cottage; John Callen, Cwmshead; George Scourfield, Griggs; Thomas John, Llantidwell and Williams John, Green Villa. The Rev Keyworth Lloyd-Williams, Buckley, son of the late Rev J.Lloyd-Williams, B.A., and Mrs Williams, Tenby, preached his first sermon at Lanteague.

Spiritually Strong

During my ministry here a successful Sunday School was held, the teachers were Mr Wm. Benjamin Davies, Mr B.G.Evans and Mrs J.Howell Phillips. The Sunday School here has been a handmaiden to the Church. I am proud to think that I had a hand in starting the United Band of Hope at Lanteague. The Band of Hope has been a mighty power for good in the district. Practically all the young people now are total abstainers. The Band of Hope meetings are also social gatherings and have been the means of drawing Church, Baptist and Congregational friends closer together. It gives me pleasure to read reports of the successful meetings you have here. The following have acted as deacons and rendered good service to the church: Wm Phillips and Thomas Phillips, Longlane, David Williams, Trenewydd, William Lewis, New House, John Callen, Cwmshead, Thomas Daniel Richards, Amroth, George Scourfield, The Griggs, and B.G.Evans, Pendeilo Cottage. The present deacons are: Messrs Ben Evans, George Scourfield, Wm Shanklin, Archibald John, and Mrs N.Williams, who is the first deaconess at Lanteague. The church, too, has been well served by its organists: Miss Beryl Phillips, Miss Katie Thomas, and Mrs Wilfred Davies.

Some of the Worthies

I shall now refer briefly to some of the worthies of Lanteague: Mr Thomas Phillips Longlane was a leading deacon and a deeply religious man. For years he entertained the ministers that came here to preach.

When the late Rev. and Mrs William Davies and their three children came to reside at Oaklands in 1895 they put new life into the church. The Rev. Lewis James wrote as follows to the South Wales Congregational Union, 'Improvement in Sunday School owing chiefly to the labours of Rev. William Davies, retired minister and his family'.

Mr David Williams, Trenewydd, did much for Lanteague. He was a very unassuming man and a man of God. He too, entertained a large number of ministers.

Mr William Benjamin Davies, Oaklands, was a helpless cripple when I first saw him. He could move neither hand nor foot but on Sunday the young people of the Church brought him here in his small carriage. He was a capable Sunday School teacher and a spiritual force in the Church. Before his health gave way he was a ministerial student.

The family at the Post Office, Amroth, rendered immense service to the church. Each one contributed towards building the Chapel.

Mr Thomas John Llantidwell also was a pillar in the Church and a very Godly man. He was one of the best men I ever met. What I have said about Mr John is equally true of Mr. Thomas D.Richards, Post Office, Amroth.

There is present this afternoon an elderly man whose name is George Scourfield for whom I have profound respect. He is the oldest member of Lanteague.

Mr Ben Evans has rendered incessant service to this Church. Since he first came to the neighbourhood he has served Lanteague faithfully and well and often in face of much discouragement. He is a man of strong Christian character, a thoughtful and considerate man with only one ambition in life and that is to serve the living God. He is certainly a minister's friend.

Mrs N.Williams, Longlane, has also rendered good service to the Church and I am glad that she was appointed a deaconess. There are other worthy people I could speak of but time does not permit.

The Rev Perri Thomas said that most of the people who built the Chapel had passed on. They were not endowed with a great education, they did not have great possessions but they built it and bequeathed it to your fold today. The fathers of Lanteague were not Christian because they had had a creed but because they had love in their hearts. The Bible was always the centre of their life, and they turned to it in joy and sorrow. As you celebrate this Jubilee their voices are coming down over the 50 years and saying 'we have given you an example that you may follow in our footprints'.

I conclude the special Jubilee Services at Lanteague Chapel. Special Anniversary Services were held last Sunday. The preacher being the Rev. D.Picton Jones, Sackville Avenue, Congregational Church, Cardiff. He delivered three excellent sermons. There were good congregations present and in the afternoon and evening the Chapel was full. In last week's report it would have been mentioned that among those who spoke was the Rev. D.Morgan, president of the Crunwere United Band of Hope. Mr Morgan said he was glad to be present with the members in celebrating their Jubilee and that he hoped that the church would go on from strength to strength for at least another 50 years."

(Little did Rev. Morgan realise how prophetic his words were. Falling attendances meant that 'Mountain Chapel' was forced to close in December 1999 just fifty and a half years after their very successful Jubilee. The chapel had served its purpose for just over a hundred years. The building has now been virtually demolished and in its place is a garden of remembrance. The vestry has been converted into a dwelling, Katelios.)

Narberth Weekly News 8 June 1939.

Air Raid Patrol Wardens in the Rural Areas – 1939

Officials who will give information (in Llanteg area):-

W.J.Allen	Rose Cottage	Llanteg
J.Y.Glanville	West Llanteg	
W.L.Glanville	East Llanteg	
W.H.James	Bevlin	Llanteg
J.S.Stephens	Summerpark (*Summerbrook)*	

Narberth Weekly News 7 September 1939.

Llanteg News – 1940

'On Furlough – Mr W.Davis, son of Mr & Mrs W.Davis of Bryneli, came home on short leave before proceeding overseas. The prayers and best wishes of all in the neighbourhood will follow him.

Whist Drive – A last whist drive before the Lenten season was held in Crunwere School on Friday last and despite the atrocious weather and the fact that it followed so closely on the previous whist drive quite a number of people turned up. The prize winners were as follows: Gents – 1, given by the Rector (gentleman's scarf) Mr E.Howells Water Goch; 2, given by Mr G.Mathias, Broomy Lake (50 cigarettes), Mr John Oriel, Rhyegwm, Whitland; Mystery Prize, given by Mrs Hughes, Mountain View (2 packets cigarettes), Mr Elwyn Davis, Bryneli. Ladies – 1, given by Mrs Allen Ruel Wall (handbag), Miss Eileen Allen Ruel Wall; 2, given by Miss Phillips, Oakland (½ dozen fruit plates), Miss E. Lawrence, Trelissey, Amroth; Mystery Prize given by Mrs Ivor Phillips, Llanteg (jug of chocolates), Miss Kate Morris, Three Wells; other prizes – cruet given by Mrs Morgan, The Rectory, Mr John Morgan, Goytre; table cloth given by Miss Griffiths, Llanteg, Master Peter Morris, Whitland; bottle of sherry, given by Mrs Bruce, Mountain, Miss Griffiths, Llanteg; box of tea given by Mrs Bruce, The Mountain, Mrs Prout, Stepaside. Other prizes which were given by Miss M.Morris, Post Office, Llanteg, and Miss Pattie Phillips, Croft-Ty (large box of chocolates and 50 cigarettes) were won by Mr Davis (*sic*), Sparrows Nest, and Mr Brinley Hodge, Red Roses. The Refreshments Committee, headed by Mrs Davis (*sic*), Garness Mill, and Miss Clarice Hodge, The Barrietts, were assisted by many willing helpers. Unfortunately Mr Fred Allen, Ruel Wall, was unable to act as M.C., owing to influenza, but a most competent substitute was found in the person of Mr William Henry James, Bevlin, Llanteg. So well did he fill the position that it is to be hoped his services may be secured for some future occasion. Thanks are also due to Mr George Mathias, Broomy Lake, for carrying out the arduous duties of doorkeeper, to Mr Collingwood, York Cottage, and to our friends of the Llanteg Congregational Chapel for the loan of their tables and forms.'

Weekly News Thusday 1 February 1940.

Llanteg Man Who Lived With Cannibals – Mr Wilfred Glanville
'News has been received from his wife in Northern Australia that Mr Wilfred Glanville, eldest son of Mrs Glanville of Ashdale, Llanteg, has joined the U.S. Navy at the age of 53 years! Before joining, Mr Glanville held an important engineering position in Northern Australia. Some years ago he came home on a month's visit here. Prior to this he formed one of an exploring party of four men who penetrated into the hitherto unknown part of the island of New Guinea. On reaching their objective they were met and surrounded by a tribe of Cannibals who had never before seen a white man, and who lived under exactly the same primitive conditions as did their forefathers of the Stone Age. For a week these adventurers slept every night in the open encircled by the men of the tribe! After their return to the Australian mainland, their adventures and scientific investigations were recorded in one of the principal monthly magazines of the USA, which obtained the exclusive copyright. This one, among many other episodes in his remarkable career, will serve to illustrate the type of man he is. Of medium height and powerfully built, he is today a 'tough guy' in the truest sense of the expression. He was an old boy of the Tenby County School, and late of Owen's Technical

College, Manchester. His old friends and acquaintances will wish him all that is best, God-speed and some day a safe return.'

Narberth Weekly News 17 June 1943.

A Real Brew – Llanteg Brewing in the 1980s at Llanteglos
'A new Welsh beer, believed to be the first produced for general distribution in Pembrokeshire, has not been named yet.

Twenty barrels a week have already started to pour from the brewery at Llanteg, and the sales distributors say that output will double within a matter of days.

The Pembrokeshire pint is the brainchild of businessman Mr Peter Johnson, who decided to take the plunge after listening to a radio discussion involving a London based entrepreneur who started to do the same thing.

So far only he and his son (Martin) are involved in brewing the real ale but jobs will be created for others when it reaches a wider drinking market throughout Dyfed.

Mr Peter George, a director of Georges of Haverfordwest who is to distribute the new ale, said that they had already had a very favourable reaction from the 16 selected pubs throughout Pembrokeshire where it had been tasted.

Georges service more than 450 outlets throughout Dyfed and anticipate a big demand for the brew. "I don't think that there has ever been one brewer like this before", said Mr George.'

Western Mail 1 July 1985.

'Eighteen months after launching a new brew for bitter drinkers the one-man company run by Mr Peter Johnson is introducing real-ale lager counterpart, which has the backing of the Campaign for Real Ale.

Mr Johnson's ale company in Llanteg is thought to be the only small brewery in Britain to produce lager in the old traditional way.

Brains in Cardiff brew their Faust Lager using the Bavarian method, but CAMRA know of no others.

Mr Johnson said "it is simply a question of going back to the basic methods of making lager as they did on the continent many years ago. Lagers are mainly carbonated, but real-ale drinkers don't like gas".

It is hoped to have the unusual lager available at pubs in West Wales next year.'

Western Mail 18 October 1986.

A footnote by Peter Johnson:- "The origins of the enterprise were a result of hearing an interview on the radio. Mr Davies Bruce, who was being interviewed, was the owner of a chain of pubs with their own 'micro breweries'. I met him at one of his establishments in Bristol and was fired by his enthusiasm. However, it was a chance meeting with Peter George, M.D. of Georges wholesale distributors in Haverfordwest which persuaded me that a brewing project could be a going concern in Pembrokeshire! In effect he said 'You brew it and I will sell it', and given their wide distribution area and facilities, I was sold on the idea.

Part of Llanteglos brewery

Photo: Peter Johnson

Unfortunately, not long after my brewery was up and running Georges was bought out by national brewers Ansells. They did agree to honour the arrangements in place at the time but this turned out to be no more than lip service. When the Haverfordwest depot was later closed, Pembs Own Ales had no choice but to go it alone. Despite selling the beer in the Hunting Lodge at Llanteglos and to a loyal band of supporters (the New Inn and Amroth Arms among them), it was always going to be an uphill task. Despite winning awards from festivals as far apart as Portsmouth and Dundee it just wasn't possible to sell enough in West

Wales due to the lack of 'Free Houses' which were not tied to the big breweries.

The brewery survived for six years, but in 1991 I had the opportunity to sell all the equipment and so the entire brewing installation was shipped 'lock stock and barrels' to Victoria in British Columbia where it was used in a 'British Pub'. It was very successful and is probably still pumping out gallons of 'Real Ale' to this day!"

Village Loses its Favourite Cobbler after 43 Years - End of an Era for Willie Boots

Willie Phillips

Photo: Willie Phillips

Willie Phillips, 78 years old, also known as Willie Boots, of Three Gates, Red Roses, had to shut up his shop in Whitland to make way for the new dental practice at Lowmead House.

Hundreds of Willie's customers, who came from as far as Nairobi to get their boots fixed, will be deprived of their favourite cobbler.

Willie, whose interest in cobbling began when he was seven, will be 79 years old in May (*2006*) and was hoping to be recognised as the oldest cobbler in Wales. He said "I suppose its time to retire but I wanted to keep going until I was 80. My father was a cobbler and the profession goes back generations in my family. I opened my Whitland business on the first Tuesday in April 1963".

In his hey-day Willie made the best boots that were sold in London – "People came from everywhere – I specialised in orthopaedic shoes because the NHS ones were unwearable. But I've also repaired a lot of fashionable ladies' stilettos in my time! People used to call into the shop regularly for a chat".

Mayor Conwil Harries will be sad to see Willie go: "….he provided an invaluable service to the community and was well respected in Whitland".

Clr Diane Evans said he will be sorely missed: "People came from far and wide to get their boots and shoes repaired by Willie. He's quite a character".

Carmarthen Journal 18 January 2006.

*Willie Phillips as a boy with his father,
Richard Phillips of
The Corner*

Photo: Willie Phillips

Willie Phillips was born and raised at Three Gates, Red Roses. He was the youngest son of Richard Phillips (of The Corner, Trelessy Lane, Llanteg) and Hannah Sharp (of Eglwys Cummin).

Albert Phillips,
brother to Richard

Photo: Willie Phillips

Matilda and Mary Phillips

Photo: Willie Phillips

Richard Phillips,
The Corner

Photo: Willie Phillips

Another family connection is that Richard's brother John Robert married Hannah's sister Lydia (two brothers marrying two sisters). John Robert Phillips and Lydia were the great-grandparents of John Lewis Tunster, Beech Lea, Trelessy Lane (Llanteg History Society Treasurer).

EXTRACTS FROM ST ELIDYR'S CHURCH MINUTE BOOK
1941-1980
(Kindly loaned by Rev'd Sarah Geach)
annotated by Ruth Roberts

1941 Easter Vestry – Mr Benjamin Jones of Heatherland re-elected as Rector's Warden (his 50th year) and Mr Alfred James re-elected as People's Warden (his 20th year).

Mr F.E.C.Wolff elected Honorary Secretary of the Parochial Church Council for the next three years.

Sidesmen chosen were:- Mr Davies Garness Mill, J.Allen, Leslie Phillips, Richard Morris, Mr D.Morris? Sparrows Nest, Mr F.Allen Rhuel Wall (*sic*), William Allen, Dai Phillips Llantidwell, T.Phillips Mountain View.

Members of P.C.C. were:- Rector and two Wardens, Mrs Morgan, Miss Griffiths, Bertie James, T.Phillips Mountain View, J.Davies Sparrows Nest, Hon. Sec. F.E.C.Wolff.

There were ninety communicants, well up on average. Two had died during the year – Mr Evan Lewis of Oaklands and Mr Benjamin Morris of Furzy Park – for many years a helpless invalid.

There were three important requirements:

1)   Either a notice board in the churchyard showing services or printed leaflets

2)   Substitution of unleavened bread (wafers) for the present ordinary bread – solely as a matter of convenience

3)   Colouring of the internal walls of church during the summer months to improve the present 'deplorable condition and appearance of the walls'.

Owing to the lateness and the blackout most of the business was held over.

May 1941 – the Bishop had suggested two buckets of sand, a stirrup pump and a ladder being kept in church as air raid precautions. The Rector would ask Alfred James to do the colouring of the church walls and cement over the bulging pieces of masonry.

September 1941 – the serious illness of Mr Davies of Garness Mill prevents him from making the notice board and instead Bertie James proposed that the Rector obtain 100 leaflets with the times of services – carried unanimously.

15th April 1942 – recorded the deaths of two faithful members:- Mrs Hodge of The Barrietts and Mr John Howell Davies of Garness Mill. Sympathy was extended to Mr Allen Oxford and Mrs Wilkins Sandy Grove who were 'laid aside with illness'.

May 1943 – the Rector regretted the frequent absence of the sidemen during services, but on some occasions this could be accounted for by the clash of duty of those in the Home Guard. Nevertheless he hoped for better attendance in future, and this also applied to the Churchwardens.

October 1943 – part of the vestry ceiling had fallen and urgently needed repair.

February 1944 – Bessie Morris, caretaker of the church, is to be relieved of her duties from Easter.

April 1944 – Churchwardens – the two well-tried men had, through increasing age and infirmity become unable any longer to fulfil their duties that they had so ably carried out in the past and in fact neither of them sought re-election. They resigned their services but we retain them in a consultatory capacity. The two new wardens were:- Bertie James (Rector's Warden) and John Davies Sparrows Nest (People's Warden). The Rector drew attention to the very bad state of the church lane and it was decided to write to the County Surveyor in Haverfordwest asking for chippings to be laid from the main road to the church gate.

July 1944 – the Rector spoke feelingly of the passing of his warden Mr Benjamin Jones of Heatherland. Paying a high tribute to the services he had rendered in the past and moved that a vote of condolence with the relatives of the desceased be passed and recorded in a letter.

The Rector also proposed a hearty vote of thanks to Miss Herbert, Assistant Teacher at the Day School, for organising the Jumble Sale in aid of the Church Renovation Fund – they raised £26 1s.

A wreath was sent to Mr Benjamin Jones, made by Tom Wilkins of Sandy Grove. It was decided that a new long table with four benches and two forms be made for the use at various functions taking place in the school. (*From July 1944 members began using envelopes for their collections.*)

February 1945 – Willie Allen proposed 10/- be handed to the Congregational Church members (*at Mountain Chapel*) for their kindness in lending their long table and forms from time to time.

April 1945 - decided that in future a wreath be sent to all deceased members of the P.C.C., Church Wardens and Sidesmen in the form of a cross. Miss F.Phillips appointed Church caretaker on £12 a year. Decided to colour the inside walls of the church with two coats of ivory.

August 1945 – the re-installation of Calor Gas – the cost per light would be £4 – and eight were needed – hoped to be done before winter.

October 1945 – Hermon Thomas promised that the light would be in by 1st Sunday in September but nothing yet. Mrs Hawes suggested cancelling the order and using the present Tilly lamps during the winter – unanimous.

Bertie James and Mr Davies Sparrows Nest went to see the Calor Gas lights at Ludchurch and were impressed. These had been installed by Mr Taylor of Pembroke Dock.

December 1945 – contacted Mr Salmon of Narberth regarding Calor Gas and told that chandeliers and brackets were not yet available.

February 1946 – Mr Wolff received a nasty accident and was not able to be present. The Rector thanked Mr Davies Trenewydd for hauling a lorry load of coal from Kilgetty to the church free of charge.

May 1946 – clearing of the church path from the field gate to the church was discussed. It was proposed to write to the County Surveyor to improve the path as was done some years ago. Also that we write to Tom Oriel, Garness, thanking him for his work on the tower free of charge.

The late Mr B.Jones had left £100 for matters essential to church purposes (executives *sic* wanted some to go towards heating).

October 1946 – the County Surveyor replied that the church approach was not a county road. A letter was received from Willie Allen saying that he was resigning as grave digger from the end of the month. The Church Social was to be held on New Year's Day 1947.

December 1946 – Llanteg Young Farmers' Club were granted use of the Schoolroom for their social on 14th January.

January 1947 – the Rector stated that the old churchyard had been turned over to the Governing Body of the Church in Wales. The vacancy of grave digger had been filled by Mr Bevan of Mountain Farm.

April 1947 – Miss Phillips The Folly finishes as caretaker of the church from 1st May.

May 1947 – the Rector made it a condition that the new tenant of the Schoolhouse should be caretaker of both the school and church. Salary for the church was £12, salary for the school not yet decided. Mrs Phelps of Milton Back was chosen.

August 1947 – estimated cost of stove, fitting it in the north aisle and stove pipe in the tower was £124 10s. Water was also coming in the west window.

October 1947 – a new Secretary was needed to replace Mr F.E.C.Wolff who had left the district. Jack Allen was selected. A letter from Mrs Evans, Pendeilo Cottage, suggested a Tilly lamp from the church be sold or given to the Congregational Church as they have lent seating for whist drives etc., over a period of years. It was decided to keep the lamps.

The following whist drives were arranged:-

Mothers' Union – Nov. 14th
Church Hall Funds – Dec. 12th
County Hospital – Jan. 9th
Church Renovation Funds – Feb. 6th
Annual Church Social – Jan. 2nd

February 1948 – the Rector brought up the state of the road across the field again. It is in a bad state – some discussion followed and it was decided that the Rector would make an appeal for volunteers to clean same.

March 1948 – the cost of the stove and fitting was up to £172 and it was decided to cancel.

The architect, due to 'misapprehension', had ordered the stove which was in transit. 'After some discussion' it was decided to accept delivery.

October 1948 – A suggestion from Mr Salmon of Narberth that larger Calor Gas containers should be installed for church lighting was not accepted but the present size retained.

The Wardens drew attention to the untidy state of the church path and decided to clean same.

November 1948 – decided in future years to purchase poppies to be placed on church altar on Remembrance Sunday – rather than make the usual donation to Earl Haig Fund (£3). Regarding the new stove – decided to write to The London Warming Company to explain its unsuitability (large fuel consumption) and asking on what terms they would take it back.

December 1948 – The London Warming Company said they would divert the stove to a church near Brecon. Mr Hawes was to write and accept the proposal.

January 1949 – members agreed that the hanging Calor Gas lamps were unsatisfactory and decided to approach Messrs Salmon with a view to changing to side lights. The Rector's Warden read an extract from the Will of Mrs Purser relating to a charity bequest to the Day School children and correspondence regarding same. A few members felt it should be divided between the children of school age as in former years (prior to the closing of the day school) while others thought that as the school was no longer in use this could not be done.

March 1949 – the path across the field was unfit for car traffic in bad weather. Mr Davies (County Councillor) should approach the Council with a view to them taking over its maintenance but in the meantime the soil covering the metalling should be removed.

April 1949 – Book of Remembrance – all present agreed that the names of those serving in the last war should be added – but it was a matter for the parish to decide.

July 1949 – Rector's Warden informed members that the Purser Charity had been vested in the Diocesan Fund.

It was agreed that the gate already obtained should be erected at the entrance to the church field and that Mr Hugh James be asked to carry out the work.

The question of space for family burials in the new churchyard was brought up and it was decided that this should be allowed if desired – providing space was kerbed. A letter had been received from the Council Surveyor disclaiming responsibility for the path across the field.

Mr Bevan resigned as grave digger.

September 1949 – Mr Phelps, caretaker, had resigned and was asked to come and give his reasons. He said the work had increased in the past year and that the salary was too low at £6 but said he would do the job for £10. It was proposed to increase the salary to £9 but Mr Phelps declined.

November 1949 – Members were informed that the cost of the Sunday school trip to Tenby totalled £10 2s which covered the bus, two meals at Tenby and a visit to the cinema.

January 1950 – a letter was read out from the St David's Diocesan Board of Finance regarding the Purser Charity which stated that the interest could not be utilised for general purposes of the Church Hall, but would have to remain in the bank until it was possible to comply with the Trust's terms.

February 1950 – decided to write to the Diocesan Board to see if the interest from the Purser Charity could be devoted to the children of the parish.

1950 Easter Vestry – Rector's Warden was Herbert James and People's Warden James Davies.

The P.C.C. was:- Mrs Hawes, Mrs Wilkins, Mrs Wilson, Mrs Davies, Miss Millie Phillips, Miss Pattie Davies, Messrs W.Allen, F.Allen, H.James, I.Bowen, A.Wilson, B.Brinsden, L.Phillips, R.E.Evans, R.Morris, J.Mortimer, T.Scourfield, J.Allen (Secretary).

Sidesmen were:- Miss M.Morris, Miss Melfa Davies, Messrs Cecil Lewis, Noel Richards, Herbert James, Norman Allen, Vaughan Wilson, Hugh James, Hugh Glanville, Elwyn Davies, Walter Morse and Brynmor Wilson.

October 1950 – The Rector convened the meeting to consider the erection of a screen at the archway which divided the main aisle from the belfry. In addition to adding beauty to the church it would help to eliminate the draught from the west window. A sketch was shown, the cost being approximately £50. After some discussion it was decided the Rector would ask Harold Thomas, Narberth, to proceed with the job.

December 1950 – proposed that a stove 1 foot 6 inches in diameter and 3 foot 9.5 inches high should be purchased from Pembroke Dock (finally ordering a 1 foot 4 inch one for price).

Font Lid,
Crunwere Church

Photo: Ruth Roberts

November 1951 – Decided to apply for a Faculty on behalf of Mr and Mrs Davies, Sparrows Nest, to enable them to erect a font cover in memory of their daughter Mrs Mabel Prosser.

Mr Howard James – in recognition of his valued service and long period as organist it was decided to make a presentation to the value of £5 (item to be chosen by Mr James).

Broomylake Stained Glass Window,
Crunwere Church

Photo: Ruth Roberts

December 1951 – The consent of the P.C.C. was readily given to Mr Herbert James, Broomylake, for the placing of a stained glass window in Crunwere Church in memory of his parents and sister.

March 1953 – the Rector expressed the great loss which the church at Crunwere had sustained by the death of Mr James Davies, Sparrows Nest, a faithful member of the P.C.C. and People's Warden for a number of years. He expressed sympathy with the relatives.

The proposed lighting of the church by electricity was discussed, and, while a few members were of the opinion that the present system of Calor Gas lighting was efficient, it was decided by a majority vote to accept the offer of the Electricity Board, provided the cost did not exceed the amount stated.

April 1953 – a meeting to discuss electricity was held. It was agreed to have electricity installed in the Church Hall and School House The rent for the School House was to increase by 2/- a week to cover capital expenditure. They were to request that the Electricity Board carry out the necessary wiring to the Church, Rectory, Church Hall and School House.

October 1953 – the heating of the church by electricity was discussed and they decided to purchase two fires and to see if they would give enough heat with the existing Calor Gas stove.

January 1954 – regarding the electric heating of the church, the Rector had accepted the offer from Pendine Establishment to install heating at the church, costing about £100. The Rector's Warden proposed that a

Plaque to Mr Benjamin Jones, Crunwere Church

Photo: Ruth Roberts

tablet in memory of Mr Benjamin Jones (*late Churchwarden*) should be erected as £100 from his estate had been left for the purpose (of heating)

– agreed. The Secretary was asked to inform Mr and Mrs Hawes (*Mr Jones's daughter and son-in-law*).

It was decided to increase the rates of rent for the School House to cover electricity from 1 January 1954 and to be £1 6s per quarter. The charges for meetings at the Church Hall were increased to 5/- with the exception of the Clinic (3/6) and for special occasions (7/6).

October 1954 – a bill for £167 11s 9d was received from Hugh and Herbert James for decorating the interior and exterior of the church and carrying out necessary repairs. The Rector asked the Secretary to record the appreciation for the quality of the work.

A letter was read from the Forestry Commission regarding the possibility of obtaining the portion of land adjoining the Church Hall for house building for their employees, but members present were uncertain as to the ownership of same and the Rector promised to contact Canon Waltern, who would be able to give some information on the matter.

January 1955 – a letter was received from the newly appointed Rector stating that the lighting at The Rectory was inadequate, as there were six in the family, and required additional lights and power points. After some discussion it was decided to pay for extra light but members felt some economy could be made regarding the number of power points.

Rood Beam, Crunwere Church

Photo: Ruth Roberts

February 1955 – discussed the erection of a rood screen at the church by Paul Davies of USA in memory of his parents. The correspondence was read by the Rector and blueprints shown – members agreed.

April 1955 – decided to insure the three stained glass windows for £800.

May 1955 – the Forestry Commission wanted to purchase the school field for a building site – discussed. Although ownership was in doubt it was decided to sell if in order – with the proviso that there should be no access through the school yard. It was decided to buy an electric fence to prevent cattle encroaching on the path on Sundays. *(Luckily for the village this 'school field' was not sold. It continued to be an overgrown area until first cleared in the 1990s and then completely reclaimed as The Old School Garden by the newly formed Community Association in the 2000s. It has now been used for Nature Workshops and B.B.Q.s and is an asset to the community.)*

September 1955 – stood in silence as a token of respect and sympathy for the passing of one of the most faithful members of the P.C.C. in the person of Mrs G.Wilkins, Sandy Grove.

A letter from Canon Halliwell Carmarthen was received regarding the ownership of the school field which stated that this would be a matter for a parish meeting. Regarding the proposed erection of a rood screen at the church the Rector read a letter stating that this could only be erected subject to certain alterations. The Rector stated that he thought that any screen would have the effect of cutting off the Chancel from the remainder of the church and had written to Mr Paul Davies stating these views and had suggested an organ would be a more suitable gift. An answer was read that Mr Davies was in complete agreement with the Rector's suggestion but would leave the decision to his relatives in Crunwere parish. Members felt it was a matter for the relatives – but as their views were not unanimous a vote was taken. A suggestion that a modified screen be erected received no support whilst the installation of an organ received a good percentage of votes. The Rector said he would let Mr Davies know.

October 1955 – it was agreed to fit a sliding glass cover to the Notice Board in the church porch to protect notices.

November 1955 – the Rector had received another letter from Mr Paul Davies. After consideration Mr Davies was not in favour of the installation of an organ because it was not of a permanent character, but he would be pleased to accept anything else which the Rector, his relatives and church members would agree to, provided it was of a permanent nature and of benefit to the church. The meeting agreed to the Rector's suggestion of a rood beam only.

January 1956 – a committee of church members was chosen to raise funds for a new organ.

February 1956 – Mrs Lloyd Jones of the W.I. pointed out that if the charge for the Church Hall was raised to 10/- (100% increase) the local branch would be forced to hold their meetings elsewhere. After discussion if was decided to raise the charge only to 6/-.

November 1956 – Mr Paul Davies accepted the figure of £329 for the erection of the rood beam and mention was made that Mrs Scourfield Owen of Whitland had kindly made a gift of an oak lectern and other furniture for use at Crunwere Church.

It was agreed a small gift should be made to Mr Desmond Scourfield in appreciation of his services as bellringer. Master Alan Mason was appointed to succeed him as bellringer.

December 1956 – discussed the bad state of the road through the field again. Decided to meet at the school to remove the water tank situated on girders adjoining the school roof which it was agreed was causing dampness to the wall of the school.

January 1957 – Mrs Hawes proposed that the carpet covering the aisles should be cleaned and dyed, preferably red, as they were a rather drab colour – agreed.

Mrs Jones proposed that wood from the old piano at the Church Hall should be converted into a small cupboard by Herbert (*James*) for holding the organist's music in church – agreed.

Permission was given to Reg Glanville to cut down a tree near the family grave.

February 1957 – tendered for work to be carried out at Church Hall – the colour should be brown.

March 1957 – decided to purchase a bottle of good quality wine to replace the one given at a recent Whist Drive because complaints had been made regarding the quality of the original bottle.

April 1957 – accepted £3 10s from Mr Z.Wazik of Milton Back for the water tank at the school.

Attention was drawn to the unsightly rubbish of treetops and hedge trimmings accumulated at the churchyard. Mr George Mathias agreed to clear this up, for which he would be paid from the churchyard fund. It was decided to purchase a litter bin for the churchyard and to erect a notice board drawing people's attention to it.

May 1957 – thanks were expressed to Mr George Mathias for his efficient cleaning of the churchyard and he was asked to continue as caretaker of the yard until Easter 1958.

Inspected work at Church Hall and School House and expressed appreciation of the work carried out by the contractor Melvyn Evans.

The question of holding some function to mark the re-opening of the Church Hall following repairs was considered but as the season was inappropriate it was decided against it.

July 1957 – the Church Wardens and Rector were to inspect the old stables and alterations to the gateway at the church.

The Secretary was to write to Mr Paul Davies as thanks for the beautiful gift of a rood beam.

June 1958 – arrangements for the induction of the Rev'd D.S.Hobbs on July 9th were discussed. Decided to provide refreshments at the Hall for visitors and others and Miss Millie Phillips and Miss Patty Davies were appointed at take charge of arrangements.

Easter Vestry 1959 – the Rector thanked the donor of the duplication machine as it is of great help in the production of the church magazine.

1961 Easter Vestry – the two churchwardens were re-elected – Herbert James as Rector's Warden and Fred Allen as People's Warden.

The P.C.C. was re-elected as follows:- Mrs Hobbs, Mrs Collins, Mrs S.Rogers, Mrs David Davies, Mrs Lloyd, Mrs James (Arfryn Lea), Mrs Oriel (Goitre), Mrs Hawes, Mrs Mathias (Greenway), Miss M.Phillips, Miss P.Davies, Miss M.Davies, Messrs I.Bowen, G.Mathias, A.Wilson, W.A.Hawes, B.Brinsden, F.Oriel, W.Allen, R.Bevan, H.R.James, D.Thomas.

Sidesmen were – Messrs C.Lewis, F.Oriel, J.Allen, G.Mathias, W.Morse, A.George, I.Bowen, H.James and W.Allen.

Easter Vestry 1963 – the passing of Mr Herbert James of Broomylake was recorded, who had been Rector's Warden for many years and a faithful churchgoer and supporter of all good causes during his life. Also of Mrs Davies Bryneli who had been a member of the P.C.C. for many years and also a faithful member.

The Rector thanked all who helped with tasks, including Howard James and Millie Phillips the organists.

October 1964 – decided to redo the electric wiring at the church and the Rector was to approach Mr R.Glanville to undertake the work.

February 1965 – the Rector said that Mr R.Glanville had kindly given the wiring and done the work for free at the church.

October 1966 – decided to hold Sunday evening services at Church Hall during the winter months.

March 1967 – the main business was the condition of the School House which was in urgent need of repair. Agreed that repairs were necessary, but because of the lack of funds it would only be possible to replace the slates on the roof at the present time.

April 1967 – it was necessary to purchase a chalice for the Holy Communion Service in the near future as at present it is in a bad state through age and usage. Also new books and a limited number of kneelers were needed.

July 1967 – unanimously agreed to purchase a chalice from the firm of F.Osborne at £136 and also agreed to purchase a lock for the Vestry door.

October 1967 – the Secretary was asked to send a letter to Mr G.Mathias sympathising with him in his continued illness.

November 1967 – stood for a minute's silence to the memory of the late George Mathias who was a faithful member of the P.C.C.

A list of repairs required at the School House was read by the Rector, but as the ownership of the School and School House was in doubt it was decided to obtain particulars regarding same.

April 1968 – the Rector read a letter from the Representative Body which stated that the Church was responsible for maintaining the hedge around the churchyard.

September 1968 – as the recent sponsored walk had been successful (in aid of Church Funds) it was unanimously decided that the Christmas Whist Drive would not be held this year.

Eveningsong was to commence at 3pm during winter months.

October 1968 – a letter had been received from the St David's Diocesan Board of Finance regarding the schoolroom. The options were:

To sell the school subject to a surveyor's report and to the approval of the purchase price by the Secretary of State for Education and Science. Or

To let the same according to the general law applicable to the letting of property by Trustees of Charitable Foundations.

Afterwards members had expressed the opinion that it would be desirable to retain the building for Church and Parish functions, but at a reasonable price. It was decided to write to the Board declaring an interest, and to obtain further particulars.

September 1969 – the Rector suggested that the £25 legacy from the late Mr T.Wilkins of Sandy Grove should be used for the purchase of a Litany Desk for Crunwere Church, which would serve a useful purpose and also be a lasting memorial. Miss Millie Phillips kindly offered to pay for an inscribed tablet for same. It was also decided to purchase two cruets for use in Crunwere Church for the Communion. The Secretary and Mrs Davies kindly donated same.

October 1969 – the Rector stated Mrs Phelps had retired from her duties as Church caretaker and, on the suggestion of Mr Bowen, Mrs Lloyd was appointed to cover the duties (at £15 per annum).

December 1969 – the main business was the proposal of joining Amroth Church with Crunwere and whether the P.C.C. had any suggestions to put before the meeting which was to be held at Carmarthen Church House on the following Monday. All members felt that this was inevitable and would have to be accepted.

1970 Easter Vestry – I.Bowen and Fred Allen were re-appointed as Rector's and People's Wardens.

The following P.C.C. was re-elected:- Howard James, Mrs Hobbs, Mrs Collins, Mrs David Davies, Mrs Lloyd, Mrs James (Afryn), Mrs Oriel (Goitre), Mrs Hawes, Mrs James (Rose Park), Mrs R.Glanville, Miss M.Phillips, Miss P.Davies, Messrs I.Bowen, F.Allen, B.Brinsden, H.James, A.George, Mr Hawes, Mr D.Davies, Howard James and J.Allen (Secretary).

The Rector hoped that attendance at services would improve. He also referred to the difficulties regarding services which arose through the joining of the parish with Amroth but hoped that with co-operation these would be overcome.

A presentation of the cash contributed by Church Members was made to Mr Howard James, Blackheath, and Miss Patty Davies, Sparrows Nest, who had recently retired as Church Organist and Sunday School Superintendent respectively, after many years of faithful service.

September 1971 – the P.C.C. meeting was held at Amroth Vicarage. The Rector and Mrs Hobbs kindly stated that they were prepared to supply sherry and refreshments for a sherry party and it was decided to hold this in Llanteg Public Hall in November (for Crunwere Church Funds).

April 1974 – the Rector expressed thanks to Mr I.Bowen for his gift of a Sanctuary carpet in memory of his wife Mrs M.Bowen, which had been dedicated by the Archdeacon on 24th February 1974. The Rector also gave thanks for the Chalice and Paten, the gift of parishioners and friends. The Rector stated that the re-wiring of the electricity installation was not the one referred to on the memorial tablet in the church (*to clarify – wiring was originally paid for with a bequest from Mr Benjamin Jones of Heatherland and recorded on a plaque in 1954. Additional work was done on the electrics in 1965 by R.Glanville, who waived the cost of materials and his labour*).

June 1974 – after some discussion it was decided to obtain 100 copies of the Burial Service, to be shared with Amroth. The Churchwarden's Staff for use in Crunwere Church had been kindly donated by Mrs Hobbs.

April 1976 – Easter Vestry – special thanks were given to the Mothers' Union who had contributed Prayer Books.

March 1978 – Easter Vestry – the Rural Dean paid tribute to the late Mr I.Bowen who had served as Rector's Warden for 15 years. All present stood in silence as a token of respect.

October 1978 – Canon Evans, the Rural Dean, informed the meeting that it would appear that Crunwere would be joined with Templeton and Ludchurch – and Amroth with St Issells. These changes, though unpopular, would inevitably have to be accepted, because of the shortage in the Ministry and ever increasing inflation.

February 1979 – members welcomed Rev'd J.B.Lewis to the incumbency of Crunwere Parish.

April 1979 – Easter Vestry – sympathy was extended to Mrs Audrey James of Rose Park on the recent sudden death of her husband Mr Geoffrey James.

P.C.C. meeting immediately after the Easter Vestry – they approved the kind offer of a carpet for the use in Crunwere Church from Mr T.Phillips who has family connections with Crunwere Church (*Tom Phillips was originally from Middleton*).

October 1979 – insurance had not been updated since 1951.

At present electric fires are used to heat the church but are not very efficient and it was proposed that four oil-filled radiators with time switches set for the early hours of Sunday morning be used. The church was to pay for the time switch and the radiators had been donated by Mr Thomas Myrtle Villa, Mrs Davies Trenewydd, and Mrs Glanville East Llanteg. Crunwere Church would donate one radiator and pay the labour charges.

Mr Thomas donated back the £40 he had been paid for the year for cutting the grass in the yard towards the heating costs.

Mr James reported that the two power points at the rear of the church should be moved to a drier safer position.

Painting – Mrs Davies Trenewydd kindly offered to donate paint and the parishioners were to provide the labour to re-decorate the church.

Carol Service – new sheets were to be printed. The children of the village were to read the lessons and to be invited back to Mrs Evans at Hydref for sandwiches and refreshments.

Midnight Service – has to be held at Crunwere on alternate years due to joining with Templeton and Ludchurch.

Church Evening – this was to be held in November as an informal meeting at the Village Hall with Mr Evans as chairman – to discuss the history of Llanteg and Crunwere.

October 1979 – arrangements for the Christmas Coffee Evening on 14th December were discussed.

Mr and Mrs H.James – Prize Draw

Mrs M.James – posters and distribute

Mrs Davies and Mrs Glanville – Bottle Stall

Mrs Thomas, Mrs Davies (Sea Breeze), Mrs Eggleton and Mrs James – Cake Stall

Mrs Dean with assistance – Side Shows

Mr Lewis, Mrs James (Wooden) and Mrs Tunster – coffee making.

The Rector suggested that the entrance fee would be donations.

It was decided to discuss the decorating of the Hall with the Hall Committee who may already be decorating for their Whist Drive.

October 1980 – a meeting was held to discuss the urgency of a need for a new organ. It was proposed to start an organ fund as one would be needed within 6-18 months. Mr Thomas was to be in charge. It was suggested that they try and get a Hammond electric organ.

EARLY 20TH CENTURY OBITUARIES
annotated by Ruth Roberts
Mr Charles Allen –
Funeral Tributes to a Popular Resident – 1939

'It was with deep regret that the residents of Llanteg and district learnt of the death of Mr Charles Allen, Oxford, Llanteg, who passed away aged 38 years. Mr Allen, who was the second son of Mrs Allen and the late Mr John Allen, Rose Cottage (Crunwere), had been unwell for the past two years and for some months past had been confined to bed.

He was a popular figure in the locality, his cheerful and kindly disposition were always in evidence and whenever a helping hand was needed Mr Allen was always there to give it. He was a faithful and active member of the Parish Church and for some years had been a sidesman and also carried out the duties of cleaner – a task in which he took a great pride. Any local event which needed support found in Mr Allen a ready helper, and he always gave his services ungrudgingly. He is survived by his widow and three children (Ivy, Connie, and Norman). The large number in attendance at his funeral amply testified to the high esteem in which the late Mr Allen was held. The mourners were: Mrs Allen (widow), Misses Connie and Ivy Allen (daughters), Mr Norman Allen (son), Mrs J.Allen Rose Cottage (mother), Messrs W. and Jack Allen (brothers), Mr and Mrs Garfield Phelps, Mr and Mrs Davies Chapel Hill (sisters and brothers-in-law), Mr and Mrs Lewis Oaklands (father and mother-in-law), Mr and Mrs Howard James (uncle and aunt), Mrs Mathias Pendeilo, Mrs Phillips Middleton, Mrs Jones Abergwili, Mrs Beynon Hayfield, Mrs Phillips Amroth, Mr Mears Whitland (uncle and aunts).'

Narberth Weekly News 5 October 1939.

Mrs Mary Davies,
Widow of the late Mr William Davies – 1928

'The death occurred on Tuesday of last week of Mrs Mary Davies, widow of the late Mr William Davies, Blackheath. The deceased, who had attained the age of 81 years, was only ill for a few days so her death came as a shock to her family. There was a large attendance at the funeral which took place at Crunwere Church on Saturday. The Rev R.Jackett conducted a service at the house, where the hymn, "My God My Father", was sung. The sad cortege afterwards proceeded to the Church, where the following took part in the service – The Rev. R.Jackett, the Rev. R.Phillips (Pendine), and the Rev J.E.Jones (Whitland). The hymns "Abide with Me" and "Rock of Ages" were sung. The Rev. R.Jackett performed the last rites at the graveside. Mrs Mathias Pendeilo (daughter) and Mr John Davies Green Acre (brother-in-law) were unable to attend the funeral. The chief mourners were:- Mr and Mrs Howard James, Blackheath (son-in-law and daughter), Mr Geo. Mathias (grandson); Mr John Davies (son), Mr and Mrs Phillips, Middleton (son-in-law and daughter), Mrs Allen, Rose Cottage (daughter), Mrs Davies, Lowmead (daughter-in-law), Mr and Mrs Beynon (Gorse), Mr and Mrs Mears (Whitland), Mrs Jones (Abergwilli), Mr and Mrs Arthur Phillips

143

(Amroth), (sons-in-law and daughters), Misses Millie and Florence Phillips and Mr Leslie Phillips (Middleton), Mr and Mrs Tom Phillips (Whitland), Messrs Charlie and Willie Allen and the Misses Nellie and Alice Allen, Mr Willie Mathias, Mrs Beynon (Gorse), the Misses Alice, Lily and Stella Davies, Mr Gomer Davies, Messrs Sidney and Jack Phillips (Amroth), Messrs Verdi, Herbert and Hugh James (grandchildren), Lawrence Phillips (great-grandson), and other relatives.

A number of beautiful floral tributes were received.'

Narberth Weekly News 22 March 1928.

Tribute to the late Mrs E.Ebsworth - 1931
Impressive Funeral at Crunwere

'Mrs Evelyn Ebsworth, of Broomylake, passed away at the County Hospital on 26th February 1931.

Lyn, as she was best known, was a great favourite with all who knew her. She was always bright and cheerful and was never so happy as when helping someone. She was a faithful member of the Parish Church of which her father, Mr Alfred James, is warden. Her death has cast a gloom over the whole neighbourhood, and the sympathy of everyone in the district goes out to the family in their great sorrow.

The funeral, which took place at Crunwere, was one of the largest ever seen in the district. The service at the house was conducted by Rev. R.Jackett. Before leaving the house, the hymn, "Lead Kindly Light", was sung. At the church the lesson was read by the Rev. R.R.Jones, rector of Rhoscrowther. The choir then sang the Psalm, and the prayers in church were read by Rev. W.L.Davies, rector of Henllan Amgoed. Rev. D.Jones, rector of Eglwyscymmin, also took part.

The chief mourners were:- Mr William Ebsworth (husband), Mr and Mrs Alfred James (father and mother), Mr Herbert James (brother), Mr and Mrs Howard James, Mr and Mrs William James (brothers and sisters-in-law), Mr and Mrs William Thomas (sister-in-law and brother-in-law), Mr Thomas Ebsworth (brother-in-law), Mrs G.Davies (aunt) and Mr Lewis James, Cardiff (uncle).

Among the floral tributes was "in loving memory of my dear wife, from Husband and Baby" (*the 'baby' referred to was Mr Noel Ebsworth*). *The newspaper article lists over 45 floral tributes which is a catalogue of most of the properties in and around Llanteg.*

The coffin was of unpolished panelled oak with silver fittings. Messrs Hubert Thomas and Son, Narberth, carried out the arrangements.'

Narberth Weekly News, 12 March 1931.
Evelyn died, aged 40 years, just three days after her only child, Noel, was born.

Mr W.J.Ebsworth, Moors Farm – 1937

'Mr Ebsworth's death came as a great shock and the heartfelt sympathy of the whole locality was expressed by the large number who gathered at Crunwere Church to pay their best tribute to one held in such high esteem.

Some of the chief mourners at the parish church were:- Mrs Ebsworth (wife) (*this was his second wife, the first being Evelyn –above - who had died in 1931),* Noel Ebsworth (son), Martha and Will Thomas (sister and brother-in-law), Tom and Edie Ebsworth (brother and sister-in-law), Mr and Mrs George Ebsworth Llanbradach, Mr and Mrs T.Ebsworth Amroth, Mr and Mrs B.Waters Kilgetty, Mr Prout Llanbradach (uncle and aunts), Roy and Freda Thomas (nephew and niece), Katie and Glyn Hughes, Terry and Leslie Ebsworth, Mr and Mrs T.Ebsworth, Ebbie Waters (cousins), Mr Alfred James, Broomy Lake (father-in-law).'

Narberth Weekly News 9 September 1937.
Like his first wife Evelyn, above, Mr Ebsworth was also to die at a comparatively young age,47 years old.

Funeral of Mr James Price John, Castle Ely Mill – 1937

'The death occurred on Saturday 18th September at the age of 78 years, of Mr James Price John of Castle Ely Mill. Mr John had not enjoyed good health for some time but was able to get about up to a few days before his death. He had spent practically the whole of his life in the district and was well known and highly respected by an exceptionally large number of people, being a regular attendant at most of the local sales and horse fairs during the greater part of his life.

The chief mourners at the parish church were: Misses Cissie and Mildred John (daughters), Mr and Mrs W.G.John (son and daughter-in-law), Mr and Mrs W.James (daughter and son-in-law), Misses Phyllis and Thelma John, Miss Winnie James, Messrs Verdun and Gwyn James (grandchildren), Mrs Williams, Cloverton (*Cilgerran*), Miss M.E.Williams and Mr J.G.Williams, Crunwere Farm.

The funeral arrangements were carried out by Mr J.H.Davies, Garness Mill.'

Narberth Weekly News 30 September 1937.

Mrs Elizabeth Raymond –
One of the District's Oldest Inhabitants – 1939

'We regret to record the death of Mrs Elizabeth Raymond, wife of the late Mr John Raymond, The Laurels, Llanteg, who passed away at the age of 89 years. Mrs Raymond was one of the district's oldest inhabitants and was predeceased by her husband 25 years ago.

She was born at Llanteg Farm and had spent her whole life in the village. For the past 36 years she had carried on a grocery business at The Laurels and took an active interest in the business up to a year ago. For the last 10 months she had been confined to bed during which time she was tenderly nursed by her niece, Miss Maggie Morris. Mrs Raymond was of a kind and generous disposition and was always a favourite with the schoolchildren who seldom went out of her shop without a packet of sweets. She was a member of Crunwere Church and a faithful attendant until her health failed her. She was a great reader of her Bible and was able to quote any passage of scripture from memory.

Mrs Raymond's funeral was largely attended. Chief mourners were: Mr James Morris Three Wells (brother), Miss Maggie Morris (niece), Misses Martha and Bessie Morris and Mr Richard Morris Furzy Park (nieces and nephew), Miss Katie Morris Three Wells, Mr William Morris Pengay Ferryside (niece and nephew). Mr Benjamin Morris Furzy Park (brother) was unable to attend owing to indisposition.

The funeral arrangements were carried out by Mr J.H.Davies, Garness.'

Narberth Weekly News 27 July 1939.

Mrs Reynolds, Belle Vue – Large Funeral at Carvan – 1933

'It is with regret that we record the death of Mrs Sarah Reynolds, Belle Vue, Crunwere, which occurred on Sunday, February 19th. The deceased was 76 years of age. Of a kindly disposition, Mrs Reynolds was held in high esteem throughout the neighbourhood. She was a faithful member of Llanteague Congregational Chapel.

Evidence of the esteem in which the deceased was held was forthcoming at the funeral on February 29th, which was very largely attended. A short service at the house was conducted by the Rev. W. Jones, Longstone. The hymn "Day and moments quickly flying" was sung at the house. A large congregation were gathered in the chapel at Carvan and feeling rendering were given of deceased's favourite hymns "O Fyniau Caersalem" and "O God our help in ages past", the Rev.

R.Jackett was unable to attend the funeral through indisposition. The Rev. W.J.Bowen, Brynsion, conducted in the chapel and at the graveside, Miss Higgon presided at the organ and played the Dead March.

The Principal mourners were:- Mr & Mrs Mason, Llanstephen (daughter and son-in-law), Mrs Oriel *(Mary Elizabeth née Reynolds wife of Thomas J. Oriel)*, Garness, Crunwere, Mr & Mrs David Evans, Rhair, Llanddowror, Mr & Mrs Dan Davies, Whitland, Mr & Mrs Edwin Waters, Quarry Park, Stepaside (daughters and sons-in-law), Mr Tom Reynolds, Llanybrie (son), Mr and Mrs Thomas Evans, Maesgwyn (brother and sister-in-law), Misses Dilys and Nelda Reynolds and Messrs Howie, Freddie, and Johnny Oriel, Misses Mattie and Margaret Oriel *(children of Thos. J. and Mary E.Oriel)*, Messrs Stanley, Willie and Alec Evans and Miss Sally Evans, Rhuir, Llanddowror, Misses Irene, Florrie, Gwen and Sarah Ann Reynolds, Llanybrie (grandchildren). Mr Tom Bayliss and Miss Bayliss, Greenbridge Pendine, Miss L.A.Bayliss and Mr Howell J.Bayliss, Winefach, Llanboidy. Mrs Evans, Llanelli, Mr and Mrs Howell Davies and Miss Mary Davies, Whitland, and Mrs Anne Rowlands and Mrs Gravelle. Mrs Glenmer Davies, Kidwelly, Mrs Joseph Berry, Whitland (nephews and nieces), Mrs Stephens, Stonyland, Gorseinon (cousin), and others.

The coffin was of polished oak with silver fittings. Mr John Davies, Amroth, was the undertaker.'

Narberth Weekly News 9 March 1933.

Death of Mrs E.Willment – 1944

'It was with regret that friends heard of the death of Mrs Mary Jane Willmot (*sic*) of 5 Goat Street, Haverfordwest, which occurred on Friday 28th April at the age of 66 years. Mrs Willmot was a native of Marros, being the elder daughter of the late Mr and Mrs G.Harries of Talyran (*sic*) Farm Marros. Before leaving the district, over 20 years ago, she was a faithful member of Zoar Baptist Church, Llanteg. Mrs Willmot was of a quiet disposition and she was held in high esteem by all who knew her. The funeral took place at Zoar Church, Llanteg, on Tuesday of last week and was largely attended. The service in the church and at the graveside was conducted by the Rev. J.T.Hopkins, Lanteague. The organist was Mr Wilfred Davies. All friends extend to Mr Ernest Willmot and family their sympathy in their bereavement. The chief mourners were: Mr Ernest Willmot (husband), Mr John Willmot, Mr and Mrs G.Willmot, Mr and Mrs Edwin Willmot (sons and daughters-in-law);

Mr and Mrs Macglave, Mrs Jeffries, Mrs B.Absalom, Mrs Horgan (daughters and sons-in-law); Mrs M.Jones (daughter) was unable to attend; Mrs M.Williams, Myrtle Villa, Llanteg, Mr W.Harries, Talyvan, Marros, Misses A.M. and S.A.Harries, Talyvan, Marros, Mr and Mrs W.Isaacs, Pendine (brothers and sisters); Ronald Willmot and Nellie Horgan (grandchildren); Mr J.Howells, Clyngwyn, Marros (nephew).'

Narberth Weekly News 11 May 1944.

Mrs E.Wolff, Crunwere – 1937

'The funeral of Mrs Elizabeth Wolff, mother of Mr Wolff, headmaster of Crunwere School, took place on Saturday.

Mrs Wolff, who passed away last week at the residence of her son, was 81 years of age, and had spent many years in the district where she was held in high esteem.

A large number of sympathisers attended at the house, where a service was conducted by the Rev. R.Jackett and the Rev. W.Barnes, Slebech. The mortal remains were afterwards conveyed by motor hearse to Brynteg Burial Ground, Gorseinon, where the interment took place.

The chief mourners were:- Mr and Mrs Wolff, Crunwere (son and daughter-in-law); Miss Sheila Wolff (grand-daughter), and Mrs Johnson (niece). A beautiful wreath was sent by Mrs Williams and the Superintendent of the Sunday School. The coffin was of unpolished oak with massive brass mounts. The arrangements were carried out by Messrs H.V.Thomas and Son, Narberth.'

Narberth Weekly News 15 June 1933.

REMINISCENCES
'Memory is the diary we all carry with us'
Margaret Carter (née Hawes)
(who sadly passed away in January 2010 aged 89 years)

Mrs Carter recalls when her father was very ill at Heatherland in 1946 and needed an important operation in London. However because of the heavy snows they were unable to travel. Their phone was not working in Llanteg so Mrs Carter had to walk to Kilgetty to send a telegram. She remembers walking on top of the snow which was so high that she could touch the overhead wires near Belview. She recalls the trek to Kilgetty and back as being "never ending".

Alun Davies – Memories of Milton Farm

Aerial view of Milton Farm   Photo: Alun Davies

"Around 1901 my grandparents, Mr and Mrs James Davies, moved from The Griggs to Milton Farm. It was here that they raised seven children – Wilfred (my father), Victor, Doris, Robert, Brynley, Lesley and Beatrice.

In 1912 my grandfather died in tragic circumstances, having fallen into the stream on the farm and drowned during an epileptic fit. My father Wilfred was just twelve years old at the time and in his first year at Narberth Grammar School. He therefore had to leave school to help his mother (who herself was only in her early thirties). Wilfred helped to run the farm and also to care for his younger brothers and sisters.

It was to be a few years before Wilfred was able to resume his studies by going to evening classes with Mr J.S.Harries, Headmaster of Tavernspite School."

When his brothers were old enough to work the farm for their mother, Wilfred, by now in his early twenties, was able to pursue a career in the Police Force in St Helens, Lancashire. Unfortunately, after a couple of years, because of health problems (asthma) Wilfred was advised to return to farming.

In 1930 Wilfred married Margaret Ellen (Nellie) Griffiths of Newton Farm, Kilgetty.

Wilfred's mother and the remainder of the family moved to Coombs Head Farm nearby and Wilfred purchased Milton Farm from her.

"There was no lane down to Milton when my father first moved there – when they first had a car his Dad has to make the lane with chippings from Gellihalog quarry. My father had a motorbike which he kept in a little zinc shed at the top of the lane."

They would go 'three on a bike' – Alan and his parents. Their first car was an Austin 7, second-hand from the minister of Llanteague and Longstone Chapels. It had a fabric body with only metal wings and bonnet. Once it was driven over a dog in the yard and it was fine afterwards – the dog that is!

"I was born at Milton on Christmas Eve 1931 and lived there with my parents until I married in 1959.

We were a musical family and could all play both the piano and organ. On Sundays I would often be playing the organ at Sardis whilst my mother would be playing at Mountain Chapel, Llanteg, and my father at Zoar, Llanteg.

I remember attending services at Mountain and Zoar Chapels as well as Temperance meetings, Band of Hope and events attended by visiting missionaries showing films.

We bought our piano from Mr Dale of Tenby (*the grandfather of Charles Dale of Coronation Street fame*). I sat many music exams at his house in Tenby.

During the Second World War 'Welcome Home' concerts were held at Llanteg school for the men and women home on leave from the services. My mother took an active part in these events and involved me in singing solos and piano duets with her. At the end of the evening a silver collection was taken and given to those on leave.

During the wartime my father was Air Raid Warden for the district and gave demonstrations to schools on how to use our gas masks. He had also been Secretary and Deacon of Zoar Chapel for over 50 years.

After the War my father formed a small committee to raise funds for a village hall. I spent many Saturdays cycling around the locality selling raffle tickets. I also remember the ex-RAF billet hut arriving in sections from Carew Cheriton. Footings were manually dug (no JCBs in those days), the site was levelled by a bulldozer provided by Wyn Lawrence, Trelessy Farm. Messrs Ellis and Richards (builders), Wisemansbridge, were engaged to build the supporting walls (approximately 4ft, so giving extra headroom). They were assisted by many volunteers. The hall was eventually completed in 1948 and on the opening night there was a dance with over 300 people. This was a popular venue for several years. My father was Hall Secretary for 18 years until he retired to Saundersfoot in 1964. At this time he was presented with a 300 day clock which was inscribed:-

Presented to
G.W.Davies
HON SEC LLANTEG PUBLIC HALL
1946-1964

This clock still has pride of place in my home.

One field at Milton was called 'Tar' but it is believed it was originally called 'Tarn'. The stream from the Rectory Hill went under Llanteg crossroads and then out at 'Norton Shute' – it ran along Milton fields until it disappeared into a pond at 'Tar'. There were lots of trout in the stream, which didn't seem to have a name and was just called 'the river'. There were many ruins behind Milton house and Rose Cottage and also along by the stream to Garness Mill. There were also some over the stream at Honeypot Hill, where damson and apple trees grew.

My aunt and uncle (mother's sister) lived at Skerry Back, my aunt would make butter for the gentry at Colby Lodge and my uncle was a gamekeeper. When they retired they went to live at the Council Houses at Summerhill.

'Black Field' was so called because of the black rabbits there. I tried to tame one once that I had caught – it didn't work!

I recall Nat Williams, Longlane, who had once been told by his wife to go and pick some damsons – she found him picking the fruit in the barn – as he'd cut down the trees and brought them in!

Tom Phillips of The Folly would travel round the village and do decorating – he was always pushing his bike with all his things on – and never riding it.

After leaving Narberth Grammar School in 1950 I served two years in the RAF, my National Service, 12 months of which were spent at Pembroke Dock. On demobilisation I joined the MOD at Pendine. In 1959 I married my wife, Joyce Rowlands, who was a Telephone Supervisor at Narberth Telephone Exchange.

Our son Ian was born in 1966. In 1971 I was posted from Pendine, on promotion, to other MOD establishments in West Sussex, Kent and

London, and on privatization, to British Aerospace in Lancashire. I retired in 1989 and returned back to my parent's retirement bungalow, Montrose, in Saundersfoot."

Elvie Davies – Memories of Crunwere

Some memories of Elvie Davies as recounted to Mrs Maureen Ebsworth in 2002. Elvie was then 94 years old and living at Llwynon, Cross Roads, Tavernspite (having previously lived at Ludchurch Farm from 1943–1959 before moving to Tavernspite). Elvie passed away in March 2005.

Callens	Maelgwyn's (of South Treffgarne, Tavernspite) grandfather Mr James had married a Callen.
Tribe	A daughter of the Williams Family, Crunwere Farm, married a Mr Tribe.
Lawrence	Miss C.Parry had taught at Ludchurch School. She married a Mr Lawrence. Her brother had kept the Post Office at Ludchurch and Mrs Lawrence became the Postmistress after he died.
Palmer	There were Palmers at Summerhill. One Miss Palmer married a man from Ludchurch (cannot remember his name).
Dalton	Maggie Dalton lived at Blaenhafod, near Three Wells. She was elderly when Elvie knew her but she was still able to ride a bike.
Hitchings	Henry Hitching lived at Pantglas, he had a son who lost a leg and died young. After Mrs Hitchings died Henry married a Mrs Hicks (a widow who had two sons, Steven and Ivor). After Henry Hitchings died his widow married a Mr Harding and they went to live at Blaengarw (they had a daughter called Ivy).
Harries	A Miss Harries of Talyfan Farm, Marros, married a Mr Williams of Crunwere Farm.
Allen	Allens lived at The Croft, Ludchurch (not called The Croft at the time). Miss Allen lived at Middleton, Ludchurch, and taught at Tavernspite School. She was a sister to Henry Allen, Gellirhenwen Farm (the father of Willie Allen the vet). Henry's sister was the mother of Maelgwyn James, South Treffgarne Farm.
Phelps	Phelps' lived at Trelissy *(Amroth)*. Eddie kept a pub at Llanddowror. Eddie's brother Bob lived at The Norton,

Amroth. Gladys Phelps (a widow) now lives at The Hawthorns, Amroth. Wyn Lawrence's (Trelissy) mother was a Phelps, her sister was the grandmother of Nora Davies (Ludchurch Farm). Sally Phelps, Trelissy, married a Mr Lawrence and lived at Blaengwaethno Farm, Tavernspite. Sally had four daughters, one of which, Brenda, married Mr Mortimer (a policeman, now retired). Sally's sister lived at The Grange.

Head Teachers   Some Head Teachers of Tavernspite School about 90 years ago are remembered as Mr Bayliss, Mr Hughes and Mr Harries.

Kathleen Davies (née Morse)

Kathleen recalls visiting The Laurels for groceries and not coming back until midnight! She would stay and have supper with Maggie (Morris), often rabbit, and listen to her records – one being 'Chapel in the Valley'. Kathleen now has the song – but this time sung by Daniel O'Donnell and it always brings back memories for her.

Kathleen also has fond memories of Miss Georgie of Oaklands (Georgiana Philipps).

Ruth Davies (née Williams)

Nanny Longlane (Hannah Williams) had to have a hysterectomy and went to Cardiff hospital, coming home on the train and returning from Whitland in a horse and trap. She had gone from the hospital in Cardiff to the station in a wheelchair. She ended up having an open wound for 18 months and was in bed, but eventually recovered from this. Hannah also is believed to have had peritonitis when younger.

Nat and Hannah Williams of Longlane are buried at Mountain Chapel. Ruth also recalls that there were many unmarked graves at the back of the chapel.

Maureen Ebsworth (née Ebsworth)

Maureen was brought up at Marros Farm and recalls an old character, Cochan Henry, who had a caravan in a field not far from Marros Church.

An old Drench Recipe for scour in cattle:-

Barbard Chalk –¼lb

Castell Soap – 2ozs

Ginger – ½oz

Rhubarb – ½oz
Spirits of Nitre – 1oz
Tincture of Opium – ½oz
(To be given in two doses.)

Memories of John (Jack) James, Clyngwyn Farm, Marros
After leaving Narberth School Jack worked for a number of years at
Trenewydd Farm, Llanteg, with his uncle Mr Williams, his mother's
brother. Jack's mother had married James James from Narberth Mill,
and after their marriage they went to live at Spite House, Tavernspite.

Jack then went to Treorchy where he found work in the mines, laying
tram lines underground. He was a great lover of music so joined the
Treorchy Male Voice Choir. He became a member of the Treorchy
Congregational Chapel and when he left the area was presented with a
number of inscribed books. After marrying Margaret James (who owned
Clyngwyn) he went to farm there.

At the end of the Great War Jack trained a choir of young men from
the Marros area who performed at a concert at Tremoilet School to raise
funds for the building of the Marros War Memorial. Later in the 1920s
he trained and conducted a mixed choir in Llanteg.

Jean Gardner (née Howells)
Jean was living at The Valley and would walk to Longstone School at
Ludchurch. She had to walk past the new phone box and would press
button 'B' in case someone had left money in it – no one else really
knew how to work the phone.

Recalling Vincent Hodge and family (who now live at St Florence)
Jean says that he told her when she was a little girl she would go on the
bus to Kilgetty to pick up prescriptions etc. but never ask for payment.

Her grandmother's diary mentions many Lewises. There were
Lewises at Blaencilgoed in 1920, and her grandfather worked at
Blaencilgoed quarry. When the Lewises sold up in 1920 he bought a
dinner service and a dresser off them, bringing them back to The Valley
on a horse and cart. Everyone was laughing as the china clinked but
there were no breakages. Jean still had the set and dresser *(and the items
were featured on a T.V.programme)*.

Kenneth George
Kenneth's grandmother at The Downs died in the 1920s. Ken remembers
hearing about her making butter to sell to Caleb Rees in Whitland - the

equipment was still in the dairy up until the war when it was given to help the war effort. Ken's mother did use the churn to make butter during the war. Arthur's elder brother sold off some of the land while his grandfather had been working away and the two never spoke again.

Gin and Martha George - sisters to Arthur George of The Downs

The Downs once owned the land where the four council houses were built (near to the school). Ken recalls that Arthur had a garden down there – the area was called the Downs Mountain. They also owned some of Bevlin fields.

Later, as the farm was smaller, they raised calves and only made butter for themselves.

What was called the Roman Road (the lane behind the Hall) which passes along by the church, ran as far as Greenbridge, Pendine.

There was once a wooden bridge near Castle Ely Mill that was washed away in floods.

Ken recalls Millie Phillips having a garden up the top of Middleton fields in the old Roman Road. Ken and his brother Clifford once took pockets of peas from there and ate them on the way home (as the Roman Road runs behind Middleton and past The Downs) – Millie followed the trail of pea pods and walked into The Downs and gave them a telling off!

The pond by Llanteg crossroads (*now filled in and would have been situated in front of The Meadow*) was full summer and winter. The Island Pond on the Laurel's Mountain went dry during the Second World

War after the area was ploughed.

York Glanville had two fields which went north from the Roman Road up to the Crosslands (from by the old Rectory west towards Ludchurch) and where there was also a large pond up at the top.

Ken recalls that Mr Phillips (The Corner), who lost a leg during the First World War, never had a wooden leg but used a crutch.

The wood to the north of the Roman Road was not always there – Ken can recall a time when his family had hay off that field.

Alwyn James

Myfanwy Lloyd, Ester Ann and Alwyn James

Alwyn was brought up at Bevlin and can recall the Island Pond on the Laurels Mountain. Here could be found buzzard hawks, lapwings and curlew, which nested on the Mountain, while moorhens would nest around the Island Pond and the Captain's Pond. There were dozens of nests in the heather. Sadly the Island Pond is now overgrown. Skylarks were always plentiful and would often have their nests disturbed during hay-making. Every year the cuckoo used to sit on the fence between Bevlin and the Laurels Mountain – he not only heard it but saw it as well. Owls would make their homes among the stones of the old kilns at Trenewydd and towards Castle Ely.

Gypsies would stop in the village on a regular basis and camp on the wide lane leading down to Rose Cottage on the right just down from the old school (now Seabreeze). Sometimes there would be two or three caravans and once camped the horses would be left to graze – but not before 'lonkering' – having their two front feet tied together to prevent them from wandering off too far.

Steam engines would also travel through Llanteg – towing their caravan behind; and often stop at Llanteg Crossroads to fill their bowsers with water from the stream that runs there.

One field between Bevlin and next to the Laurels Mountain was called Pit Field. The pit was so large it covered three quarters of the entire field and made it too difficult to mow. Alwyn recalls when living at Bevlin it would sometimes be cut with scythes to stop it from getting overgrown. It is not known whether this was a natural dip in the field (as so many also were in neighbouring properties such as Middleton etc.) or whether it had been dug out years ago for some purpose. Mr Ted Collinson, who later lived at Bevlin, used the road widening of the main A477 as an opportunity to get surplus soil and fill the pit in. There is probably no evidence on the ground that it ever existed now, but viewed from aerial photographs (such as Google Earth) the outline of the large pit is still plainly visible.

The Hall Field (as it was known), west of the Hall, would regularly need to have a dip filled with stones, another was in the lane behind Craftie, plus one behind what was then the shop at The Laurels. It appeared that these dips ran in a line across the parish and may have been following the course of an underground stream which flowed towards Milton and Marros.

Audrey James (née Rowlands)

Geoffrey and Audrey James

Photo: Audrey James

Audrey has lived at Oaklands and Rose Park in Llanteg and remembers the Hodges of The Barrietts once building a cart in the shed – which ended up being bigger than the doorway to get it out!

When she lived at Oaklands and her son Roy was about five or six (in the mid 50s) he would play outside in the road as cars echoed and you could hear them coming a long way off. Also, later on, Roy would walk down to Maggie's shop at The Laurels and there was never any worry that he would not be safe.

Fossils were found at Rose Park in the 1970s, one with a toad inside which went to Aberystwyth College for testing. There were snails imprinted in some of the rocks.

Betty James (née Shepherd)

Betty married Herbert James of Blackheath, and Betty's mother Barbara and Clara Allen were first cousins. When Clara went on holiday from Cardiff she met her husband, Herbert John of Castle Ely Mill. They moved to Mexico and had three sons – Beverley, Arthur and Leslie. Herbert died in a tornado accident in Mexico and the family returned to Britain. Clara died young aged just 38 years and Beverley and Arthur were brought up by their aunts Cissie and Mildred who moved to Woodfield. Leslie lived in Cardiff. Arthur later went to live in the Midlands and Beverley moved to Gloucester.

Hugh James

Hugh was born at Blackheath and remembers:-

Village Ponds – The pond that was once between Middleton and Blackheath was allowed to be filled in by his brother Herbert when the main A477 was being redone. It was here that the circus stopped to water their animals when Hugh was a young boy. Hugh recalls that when they cleared out Blackheath pond they would need two or three cartloads to move the waste and spread it on the Lower Field across the road.

He remembers Middleton pond as being unusual because sometimes it would be full in dry weather and very low in wet weather (*this is two fields north of the house and next to the right of way that is called The Roman Road*).

The Captain's Pond had willows and moorhens.

The Island Pond was on the right-hand side of the path that goes from Mountain Chapel to the old school across The Laurels Mountain. It was not very deep but had a little island in the middle, now overgrown. Hugh can recall skating on it as a boy.

Hugh recalls that when the water was piped under the main road at the crossroads near the garage, he and his brother Verdi would crawl through the pipe under the road as it was very large (*now covered by a large grating to prevent young boys doing this!*)

Hugh remembers that the lower field at Broomylake was one of the first in the area to be mown for hay – usually in early June.

Hugh recalls William Richards who lived at Sandy Grove in the 1920s/ 30s – he worked with Howard James, Hugh's father. Sandy Grove then had very high ceilings – but no upstairs. Mr Richards had an old valve radio in his bedroom window (the room nearest the road). Hugh would go to listen to football matches (and has been an Arsenal supporter ever since).

Alfred James, Hugh's grandfather, would carry voters down to Amroth School for voting in elections – however, he would leave people behind if they did not vote Conservative!

There was at one time a lovely trap at Middleton – black with green stripes. This was used to collect Millie Phillips (from Whitland) when she returned home ill from Barnwood House Hospital where she had been working (in 1920s).

It is believed that Blackheath was built on round settlement foundations. This had been more visible previously but numerous road improvements has destroyed most of the circular shape.

Hugh remembers that there were searchlights in the field opposite the Rectory (now Crunwere House) during the Second World War.

Hugh cannot recall any graves at the site of the original Mountain Chapel (at the end of The Claypits towards Bevlin) but he does remember walls about 3-4ft high. Hugh was the person who put up the existing rood beam and back wooden reredo in Crunwere Church. He also cut down the font and moved it (from the front by the piano) to the back of the church.

Hugh would also do grave lining and lined one in Whitland yard for the funeral in 1963 of Mary Phillips (*Ruth Roberts's grandmother*) with a black cross at the head.

The incident of Mr Davies's death at Oaklands in recalled. Hugh said the bull was in a dip behind Oaklands – which makes them go mad (is it the echoes? A similar thing had happened at Eastlake). The maid had tried to get the cows in for milking but the bull was wild – so she had gone back for Mr Davies. He was being tossed in the air when another William Davies (Hugh's grandfather from Blackheath) had heard the commotion while walking back from work at Gellihalog. A dog then distracted the bull and enabled the injured Mr Davies to be rescued – but he died from his injuries. *(See note on inquests earlier in the book.)*

The late Ray James (née Davies)

Ray stated that reading one of our books brought back lots of memories.

'It all came about by my marrying a Llanteg boy, who I met at an Eisteddfod at Tavernspite Village Hall, back in 1941. (*Ray married Richard Edgar James (Dick) in 1945, the son of Bridget Lilian James née Phelps.)*

It was wartime, with rationing, coupons and petrol being very scarce. So we had to hire a taxi from St Clears so that the radius was no more than 10 miles. We were married at Ciffig Church, the one Alfred James restored in 1890. My husband was born at Goitre; later the family moved to Eastlake when he was two years old.

My mother-in-law was born in 1893 and used to reminisce about her days as a young girl in Trelessy. She remembered that during the First

World War the shire horses were taken from the farms to work with the army. It was a very sad day to see the strongest and best horses taken – not to return. The family also lost a brother, Peter Phelps, during that War. She also recalled a family living at the Factory, just down the lane, who would borrow their pony and trap to fetch the midwife from Narberth when a baby was due. Another of her memories was of when the first phone box came to Llanteg: a farmer had a very sick cow and the vet lived in St Clears. So the farmer thought he would try the phone box. No luck – he just could not make head nor tail of it. So he asked a lady who was walking past if she knew how to use it. Oh yes, came the reply – but it's a long way to St Clears, so both of us will have to shout together! She believed that a good laugh was better than a bottle of medicine. I recognise lots of people from the books: so many have passed on now – each one a diary of their own.'

Roy James

'When we lived in Oaklands mum and dad kept pigs, and once a year a pig was killed and cured (salted) - this provided bacon for most of the year. I was usually in school when the pig met its end and disappeared from the sty. Also dad would grow vegetables which he spent ages cultivating, since most of our food came from the garden.

Geoffrey James,
Roy's father

Photo: Audrey James

In 1958 we moved to the newly-built bungalow at Rose Park. To pay the mortgage mum and dad let the bungalow to summer visitors, whilst we moved into a converted railway wagon and chalet in the garden. It was a novelty for us, since we got to move house twice a year, but it couldn't have been fun for mum or dad, although over the years we met some wonderful friends!

In the early '60s we started taking in touring caravans, and often in those summer evenings our Welsh and English visitors played football against our Dutch and German visitors in our version of the World Cup. In the summer of 1966 the railway wagon was full of visitors when England hosted the World Cup, mum made sandwiches and tea, since all were welcome! Later in 1969 the chalet was full to capacity again when Neil Armstrong said those famous words "That's one small step for [a] man, one giant leap for mankind". In the summer we would build a tree house in the Barriett's woods, or a go-kart made from old pram wheels was used to record the fastest run down Rose Park lane. In the winter a sheet of corrugated zinc was made into a toboggan, and there was a competition for the fastest run on a hill at Craig y Borian woods.

A friend of my father (Mr. Goldsworthy) would call in for a cup of tea from time to time. He was an AA patrol man, who wore a thick brown woollen uniform with brown leather boots, and he rode a motorbike with a yellow side car. My father and he would tease each other with outrageous stories. On one occasion a small hole appeared at the bottom of our road, and my father told Mr. G. that he had seen a thunderbolt strike the main road. A few hours later there was a report on BBC Radio Wales saying that a thunderbolt had struck the road in Llanteg, traffic was being diverted and the Council were repairing a huge hole which had appeared in the road. We later asked the BBC for a recording, and still have it to remind us of that day when Llanteg was famous!

Before I was old enough for school my mother would take me to Whitland every week to visit my great-grandparents, and to pay the mortgage at the bank. We had to walk to either Red Roses or Kilanow Cross to catch the bus, and if we missed the bus we had to walk since we didn't own a car.

In the early days at Oaklands there was no mains water supply, so my parents collected the rain water from the roof in a large tank, which was used for washing; whilst the drinking water was carried by my mother from the well at Mountain Farm, then boiled and cooled. My father worked for the Ministry of Defence at Pendine (Proof and Experimental), and would leave for work at 6am, being picked up by Ebsworth's bus and returning at 6pm. Any spare time he had was spent cleaning the land at Rose Park. At weekends and school holidays we would be picking stones and cutting hedges with Dad; it all seemed a never-ending task.

Sometimes mum took me with her when she picked or set potatoes for Leslie Williams of Crunwere Farm, and I would play in the fields all day till she was ready to go home and make our evening meal. In the late '50s my grandmother had a TV, although compared with today's giant flat plasma screens it was microscopic, and black and white of course. So on Saturday evenings we would all go to watch Quatermass and the Pit (science fiction horror) on a 12" screen - the alternative was to listen to the radio which was pretty poor!

In the '60s I remember we had a Friesian cow called Blackie who always seemed to want to get the better of my father at milking time - when she was being hand milked she would kick the milk bucket over or put one foot into the milk! On one occasion dad was milking Blackie with an assembled audience of summer visitors looking on, when Blackie flicked dad's hat off his head with her tail (it landed right side up), and she then proceeded to fill it to the brim with piping hot dung. We never let him forget that day when Blackie was at her very best and the talk of the herd!

I also recollect that every Tuesday and Thursday the Co-op bread van would call and drop off all the stale bread from the Co-op at Kilgetty for the pigs.

At the time my dad had a cow called Annie, she was named after my grandmother (for some reason best known to dad), and she had a fondness for bread, amongst other things. So every Tuesday and Thursday you could be certain that she would make her way to the field nearest the main road to collect a stale loaf of bread from Dai the Bread, she seemed to have a sixth sense and was never late! Annie was also partial to other tasty morsels. I remember on one occasion when dad called out John Bowen the Vet one late night since we thought old Annie had some incurable disease, only to find that she was drunk. Later in the week dad discovered Annie shaking an apple tree with her bottom and eating all the fallen apples, I still remember her staggering towards the milking parlour that evening, and her milk was a bit special!

163

Peter James   Photo: Roy James

My first recollection of Peter James was in 1959 when my father and I visited his home at White House Mill, Lampeter Velfrey, where he had built his own generator to supply power to the house. At the time the Express Newspaper was offering £10,000 for the first person who could fly over a set distance and altitude under their own power. Peter had hand-carved a propeller from some rare African timber (or so he said), and mounted it all on the front of a bicycle to test his theory that he could create enough power to win the prize. Apparently the test was not a complete success, and after some minor cuts and bruises he decided to give up his idea of flying! Uncle Peter, as we called him, was not our real uncle, but at that time family friends were called aunty or uncle as a mark of respect. However Peter was dad's cousin and over the years he became a real uncle to us all. Peter was a small man with definite ideas, all believable, and backed up with his unique brand of science and logic. Peter was a bachelor with somewhat eccentric ways but with the ability to resolve or have a logical answer for most problems, having as he used to say "studied Medical or Electronics" or whatever was being discussed. He had in fact no qualification whatsoever, since he was born into a time when only the privileged could afford the luxury of further education. He was the fourth eldest son of a family of fourteen children, having been brought up at Telpyn Farm and educated locally at Amroth School. His father had been a victim of mustard gas from the First World War, and suffered ill health for the rest of his life, so the job of bringing up this large family weighed heavily on the shoulders of his mother and elder brothers and sisters. However the respect and love for his mother remained with Peter to the end of his life, and as he told us on many occasions his mother would carry a sack of flour on her head every week from the West Cambrian store (adjacent to The Laurels) to Telpyn, where she would make bread for the family.

Peter had a dry sense of humour that would leave you with thoughts that perhaps life is not at all what it seems. On one occasion in the mid-sixties my father and Peter went on a trip to Essex in order to buy some parts for a tractor. Considering this was pre the Severn Bridge and sat-nav, they managed to get lost on their way back and on the wrong side of the Severn. The sun was low on the horizon, so Peter decided that since the sun set in the West and was also the view he had from his kitchen window, they would head towards the sun. They ended up in the South West of England!

In the 1960s Peter drove a green mini van and would store his tools and equipment in the back of the van; this was at a time when there was no thought of stealing. I once saw him hunting through the contents of the van in search of a spanner, but to no avail, he then remarked "a spanner will hide from you just to aggravate you"!

On one occasion Peter was having a conversation with a German holidaymaker about people from his early life, relating stories about "Ben Eastlake" and "Nat Longlane". Needless to say our German visitor could not understand English, but this did not fluster Peter! Despite having no qualifications, Peter had developed many skills, and was a good electrician and engineer, with his workshop full of his creations with a lathe and milling machine made from various spare parts from motor vehicles and electric motors.

Sadly on April the 9th 1994 after a long illness Uncle Peter finally left us to continue his journey - he certainly gave us lots to think about. Good luck Pete!'

Kay Scourfield (née Scourfield)

*Dorothy May Scourfield
(née Evans) -
believed to have been taken
on her 21st birthday -
4 March 1941*

Photo: Kay Scourfield

Kay's mother was a friend of 'Betty Bevlin' (Betty James). Kay's parents lived at Belview, Llanteg, with their children – Bernard, Eileen and Gareth, before moving to Ludchurch.

Kay's uncle, Evan Llewellyn, was engaged to Miss Knowles (a teacher at Crunwere). Unfortunately he died a week before their wedding but Miss Knowles kept in touch with the family.

Avrenah Tremlett (née Jones)

Avrenah's mother was Lucy Jones (née Davies), who had been brought up at Blackheath. Lucy left home at thirteen years of age and went into service, working first at Crunwere Rectory, Sodson Manor, Ferryside (as a companion to a Miss Phillips) and later at Abergwili where she was to meet her future husband who was the village blacksmith. Lucy at one time worked at Brynmerddin (one of the 'Big Houses' in Abergwili), they would all be in their white aprons waiting for the coaches to arrive. They married in 1916. It was at Abergwili that Lucy contracted TB, and her employers kindly paid for her to go to a private hospital on Dartmoor for two years. Here Lucy was out in all weathers and would be breaking stones with the convicts (but not allowed to speak to them!) However this harsh regime worked and Lucy came home completely cured.

Lucy married William Jones and they had two children: Avrenah and Dewi. Avrenah's brother died aged five and half of meningitis when she was only two and a half and she recalls, "I was an only, lonely child. That is why I always spent the August holidays in Blackheath (*with her Aunt Emily and Uncle Howard James*), travelling down on Ebsworth Buses, where I was spoilt rotten!!

L. to R: Emily James, husband Howard, niece Avrenah Jones, son Hugh and sister Lucy Jones (mother of Avrenah)

Although I had my jobs to do helping Aunty Em (such as the shoes for Sunday – all the shoes the men had worn at the weekend were laid out on the little wall for me to clean), she was glad to have a girl around. I enjoyed doing other things to help, especially if we were going off on one of our visits. Every year before I arrived Aunty Em would buy a pretty cup and saucer for me to use and then take home with me. During those Augusts the weather was so hot with hardly a shower – happy days. I slept with her and we used to read 'Red Letter' fiction magazines by candle light in bed". Avrenah would also watch as Emily filled in her diary. Avrenah had been ill as a child at about 12 years of age when she had to have an appendix operation. Emily also loved to curl her hair with pipe cleaners (Avrenah's mother was not pleased!). Emily James herself had three sons, Verdi, Hugh and Herbert, and no daughters. "I would sit with Herbert on a box by the centre upstairs window in Blackheath and we would watch the sea, especially in a storm when we might see flares. We used to go off for the day visiting Broomylake, Rose Cottage, Milton Back, Pendeilo, Cwmrath, and Upper Mead, especially for Amroth Big Day.

I loved walking to Church on Sunday and I used to hang on the gate (*at Blackheath*) in the evening watching the 'monkey parade' of young men and women walking by (*doing their courting*). Joan and Lawrence Phillips (from Whitland) would also be staying with their aunts and uncle and grandmother at Middleton (*their grandmother Kitty Phillips was a sister to Emily and Lucy*) and we had lots of fun making reed boats to sail on the pond or playing 'shop' with the cattle and chicken feed in the barn. We would all roam the fields up to Bountyland (*to the north of the footpath behind the Hall and Crofty),* there were plenty of places to play in the top field at Middleton, down the Stoney Road, down to Maggie's shop (The Laurels) or down to Oaklands to see Miss Georgie and buy a bag of crisps. I once fell off a tree at Oaklands and swore Hugh and Herbert to secrecy as they weren't supposed to be down there climbing trees.

The gate pillars of the three-corner field were large and had a flat top. Joan (Phillips) and I would sit there and collect car numbers, it took us ages to make our lists, and also see what different types of lorries were about.

*Howard and Emily
James
outside
Blackheath*

Aunt Em was a great teller of ghost stories, making my skin creep as we all sat around the fire by lamplight on a Sunday night eating cold potatoes put on the fire and eaten with home-made butter. They were great times, never to be forgotten. I feel sad now when I pass the modernised Blackheath and Middleton. Hugh James, Arfryn, and I are the only first cousins left from the Davies family of Blackheath."

Avrenah's daughter Marilyn is married and now lives at Pleasant Valley.

George and Lucy Mathias (twins) were Avrenah's cousins and were brought up by their Aunty Emily at Blackheath. Lucy had a club foot and had to attend hospital in London. In later years Lucy went to live at Corner Park. Avrenah's Aunty Kitty (Catherine Phillips, Middleton) visited her sister Lucy at Abergwili when she was 92 years old, travelling from Llanteg by bus and walking from Carmarthen out to Abergwili.

The late George Vincent

'The book (*Llanteg – Turning Back the Clock*) transported me back to the early thirties when I often spent my annual seven week summer holidays staying with my beloved grandparents – George and Susannah Scourfield of Milton Back Farm.

During later years my grandfather worked for Pembrokeshire County Council, being responsible for drainage, hedge and drain maintenance on that part of the A477 from Stepaside to the boundary milestone just beyond Reg's Garage (*possibly the county boundary marker on Castle Ely Bridge rather than the milestone just past the garage*).

The family attended the Congregational Mountain Chapel, which has now been demolished to become a Memorial Garden. Both my grandparents are buried in the small graveyard.

My grandfather loved his pipe and smoked 2oz of Ringer's Shag each week, plus anymore that his children would secretly smuggle to him when Granny wasn't looking!

My grandmother was chairbound in her later years and always wore a Welsh shawl around her shoulders and sat in her basket chair from which she ruled the roost. As her grandson I was expected to read aloud to her from the Bible every evening, at exactly a quarter to nine. In addition to this each Sunday morning upon returning from divine service I had to provide her with chapter and verse of the morning service.

At one time or another the family lived at The Moors, Stanwell Villa and Milton Back.

Milton Back was two fields away from Milton where Wilfred Davies lived. Many an early morning he would take me with him to pick up the trapped rabbits. I would also have a ride on his motor bike to Zoar Chapel on Sunday afternoons. I spent many evenings at Milton and was guided back to Milton Back across the fields by a candle left burning in an upstairs side window. Wilfred married and took up residence at Milton. His mother and sister Beatrice moved to Cwmshead and often invited me there at harvest time for the most wonderful suppers.

My son bought a caravan from Beatrice and our family once again spent many happy hours at Pendeilo Park.

I recall a Mr Wolff and his daughter Sheila. He was the schoolmaster and lived in the Schoolhouse, which was about a quarter of a mile from Reg's Garage. Each month the travelling library would deliver a box of books to the school and we were allowed to draw out two at a time under the direction of Mr Wolff. My Aunty Gwaldys and Uncle Affie lived at the Griggs Farm near the Folly Cross with my cousins Hilda and Hugh.

Coming from an urban environment (Port Talbot) into your lovely rural countryside was truly entering "God's own country".'

CHRISTMAS CUSTOMS
by Ruth Roberts

Questionnaires were sent out after Christmas 2006 and some replies relating to how Christmas and other holidays were celebrated are recorded below.

Betty Bevan (née Davies)
(Brought up at Trenewydd, Llanteg – date of birth 14 June 1923)
Betty recalls having a fir tree at Christmas, as well as holly, ivy and bought mistletoe. Decorations were bought paper ones. Goose was eaten at Christmas and presents would be wrapped in coloured paper and opened on Christmas morning – she recalls boxed handkerchiefs (*don't we all*) and nuts. Betty remembers always having plenty of food at Christmas but the worst part was that the farm work still had to be done – milking etc.

Regarding other holidays – Betty recalls getting chocolate Easter eggs and sometimes new clothes for Easter. Her father would buy sparklers and jumping jacks for November 5th.

170

Margaret Brinsden
(Brought up in King Edward Street, Whitland –
date of birth 14 October 1942)

Margaret recalls home-made decorations of paper chains and lanterns, with the family having a Christmas tree which was put up on Christmas Eve. Christmas cards were sent with scenes of snow, robins and churches. Presents were opened early on Christmas morning and Margaret recalls having a pretty doll and a doll's pram – she named the doll 'Rosie'. In her Christmas stocking she would have half-a-crown, nuts, orange and an apple. Mince pies and sherry were put out for the lucky Santa.

They had a chicken dinner 'with all the trimmings' and pudding with brandy sauce. Margaret remembers that 'all my memories of Christmas were good ones'. She sometimes went carol singing, mostly in the street where she lived.

At Easter Margaret had small chocolate eggs – 'which were put in our egg cups on the breakfast table'. New clothes and shoes were also usually had for Easter.

On November 5th there was a bonfire at the end of their street, plus fireworks. Children from the street always made the guy. The fireworks were bought from a shop in King Edward Street.

The late Margaret Carter (née Hawes)
(Brought up in Haverfordwest – date of birth 8 March 1920)

Mrs Carter recalls having paper chain decorations (some home-made) and Christmas cards would have mainly winter scenes, plus some with robins. Father Christmas was believed in for years as 'I didn't want not to!' and is remembered as a 'jolly gent'– the family left out sherry and mince pies for him. Christmas presents were wrapped in coloured paper and one, a baby doll, is remembered.

Church was attended on Christmas Day and there would be goose for lunch, with all the trimmings, and crackers. Mince pies would be taken to the Alms Houses.

Mrs Carter remembers Christmas as 'always a very happy time' and has no bad memories.

At New Year the family had a large party of forty people ('always the same ones') for a buffet supper and they would play 'Murder' – and as the house had a front and back stairs it was ideal. There would always be a 'first footer'; who came in with a lump of coal.

Mrs Carter recalls, 'One of the things we did every year when we were exceedingly young was to put on a "show". We used to make up and act a concert - this we did for many years and asked the (poor!) parents to come and watch and they had to pay 6d to come in. The proceeds my father used to send to the Sunshine Home for Blind Babies. I found out, years later, that he continued to send them a donation for many years, which was a nice idea'.

Noel Davies

(Brought up at Bryneli, Red Roses – date of birth 22 December 1926)
At Christmas Noel remembers the decorations as being 'holly, gathered from the hedges, and draped over pictures, mantelpiece etc.'. He does not recall other decorations or any cards.

Noel put up a stocking and believed in Father Christmas 'who came down the chimney'. Presents were opened on Christmas morning and were 'small things – I remember a gun which fired cork "bullets". I was so excited and my aim so poor, that, unintentionally, one of the "bullets" landed on my mother's spectacles – no harm done!' Noel believes the presents would have been wrapped in brown paper. No food was left out for Santa.

Christmas dinner was a duck –'cooked to perfection', there were no sprouts but they had oranges, dates, pudding, cake and mince pies.

Noel has no bad memories of Christmas and his best memories are 'of waking up Christmas morning early and finding my stocking (hung on the bottom of my bed) full up of oranges, nuts, dates etc.'

Noel would go carol singing at New Year 'not at Christmas!' and would go New Year's Day morning, mostly singing 'While Shepherds Watched Their Flocks by Night'. 'It was considered lucky if a person with black hair crossed the threshold on New Year's morning, so with my jet black hair I was always warmly welcomed into the house and given fruit and/or 6d or a shilling. This was in keeping with the Welsh tradition of Calennig – a New Year's gift'. He would go to Crunwere Farm, Oxford and Castle Ely and then work his way up to Red Roses – 'I didn't go to the Llanteg homes'. As older boys ('no girls involved as I recall!') they would go round the farms on their bikes after midnight singing carols, money was then thrown down from a bedroom window.

For November 5th they celebrated with fireworks bought from Whitland –'sparklers and jacky jumpers were our favourites'.

Another 'tradition' that Noel recalls was 'that those starting at

Narberth County Intermediate School were given a brand new bike. Mine was a B.S.A. costing £5 in 1937 and was fitted with the Eadie Coaster back pedal brake which was very efficient and ideal for displaying skidding tricks!'

Elizabeth Dee
(Brought up at Pontypool - now living at The Valley, Llanteg – born on 14 August 1944)

A fir Christmas tree was put up about a week before Christmas, always in the front room window facing the road so that it could be seen by passers by. 'We made paper chains and painted small Chinese lanterns. We cut out snowflakes from white paper and hung them from the ceiling with cotton. We had shop bought glittery set pieces (churches, snow scenes) to pin to the walls and tinsel and tree decorations for the tree. We also made Father Christmas and snowmen out of toilet rolls with crepe paper and cotton wool. We had some small painted wooden toys, glass ornaments and balls and hand-made paper ones we had coloured and cut out ourselves, plus ribbon bows.' There would also be holly and ivy which they had from a relative's garden.

Christmas cards were sent and the pictures were of snow scenes, Father Christmas with toys, Victorian children, robins and religious cards.

'I believed in Father Christmas until I was about 12 years old. We were taken to see Father Christmas every year in a beautiful Grotto in a big store. He was always "the real one" and filled us with awe and excitement.' A mince pie and milk would be left out for Santa on Christmas Eve.

'When we were old enough I used to enjoy going to the midnight carol service on Christmas Eve.

My sister and I had twin beds in our room and whoever woke up first Christmas morning woke the other one up to see if Father Christmas had been. We used to wriggle our feet up and down in the bed in the dark to hear if there was any crackling paper or weight from the stocking laid on the end of the bed. We were so excited we rarely went back to sleep. One of my mother's stockings would be hung on the end of our bed. Presents were wrapped in wrapping paper and there would always be a tangerine in the toe of the stocking, wrapped up in silvery paper. We usually woke up early and were allowed to open one present each before 7am. Then my sister and I took our stockings and presents from the end of our beds and went and opened them in our parents' bedroom, sitting either side of their bed. Our main present from them was always underneath their bed – which was opened after our stocking presents. My most memorable present from them was when I was about 10 years old and in my first year of Grammar School and I would have to pass a newsagents and toy shop every day to and from school. Sometime before Christmas there was a beautiful bride doll in an enormous box and every day after school I would tell my mother about this doll with curly brown hair, gorgeous white dress and veil and with red roses in her bouquet. I was broken-hearted and in tears one day in December when the doll had disappeared from the window. I told my mother all I wanted was a bride doll for Christmas – exactly like the one in the shop! Imagine my joy on Christmas morning when I found my main present wrapped with a big bow was none other than my beautiful bride doll!'

There were small crackers on the tree and always a big cracker in their stockings. There would also be crackers on the table for Christmas dinner. For dinner the family had turkey, or sometimes goose. There would be brussels sprouts which Liz disliked, there was also 'usually too much of the sweets and chocolates out of our stockings'.

Liz's best memories of Christmas are 'the excitement and magic of the Christmas season – the build-up to Christmas Day and all the Christmas projects and concerts at school. After opening our Christmas presents we would meet up with all my aunties, uncles, and cousins at my grandmothers where trestle tables were laid end to end to accommodate us all for Christmas lunch. My mother's sisters would all be laughing and joking and all my hearty uncles would join in with festive cheer – especially when all the children found silver threepenny bits in their puddings!'

The worst memory of Christmas was 'being in hospital for six months at the age of four years and not being allowed to see my parents for weeks and weeks'.

Liz went carol singing every year - 'a group of us would go and also take our musical instruments. We played and sang about four different songs at each house. I'll never forget we were actually given a half crown by a lady at one house! Usually we would only go within a radius of half a mile from home'.

Liz was not allowed to stay up on New Year's Eve but the family would have New Year's Day lunch with aunts and uncles or they would come and visit her family.

At Easter there were chocolate Easter eggs and also Easter cards.

'Sometimes there would be a new outfit to go to church. One year my mother's friend made my sister and I blue bonnets trimmed with flowers – I still remember them – they were very pretty. I remember going to church and being given palm crosses on Easter Sunday. We weren't allowed to play outside the garden on any Sunday. On Good Friday we always had fish, no meat was allowed. Also on Mothering Sunday there would always be little bunches of violets in church for the children to give their mothers.'

November 5th was celebrated with fireworks, bonfire plus a guy. 'My father bought the fireworks for us. Sometimes we went to a big display. I remember once a "jumping jack" seemed to chase us around the garden as it zig-zagged after me! We also had cocoa and sticky toffee apples.'

Noel Ebsworth
(Brought up at Pleasant Valley, Stepaside - with Llanteg connections – born 23 February 1931)

Few decorations are recalled due to the Second World War. Noel remembers a holly bush used for a tree, with paper home-made decorations and the house decorated with holly.

Christmas cards are remembered and were mostly religious.

Noel would put up a stocking, and gifts remembered are a football and football boots which were opened on Christmas morning – 'I promptly kicked the ball through the window!'

They had home-made crackers and ate chicken for Christmas dinner, with sprouts, dates, puddings, cake and mince pies. Church was attended on Christmas Day.

Noel's happiest memories are of having 'family and friends at home'. His worst memories are of wartime shortages – and of 'breaking the window with my football!'

Noel would go carol singing 'approximately a one-mile radius from home'.

Christmas is remembered as 'always cold and hoping for snow'.

Over New Year Noel would stay up until midnight and then go 'first footing' to neighbours – taking 'a lump of coal'.

At Easter an egg decorating contest is recalled and Noel sometimes had chocolate eggs, sometimes painted ones. Having new clothes for Easter was 'difficult during wartime as one needed clothing coupons'.

Apples were bobbed at Hallowe'en but not much else due to the 'blackout'.

Delmi Evans
(Brought up at Velfrey Road, Whitland - with Llanteg connections –
born 2 March 1935)

For Christmas decorations Delmi recalls 'interlocking rings made from coloured paper and strips of silver paper from Woolworths plaited into concertinas'. There would also be paper streamers corner to corner at home. There was no Christmas tree but the family did have holly and send cards – robin designs are remembered.

A stocking was put up on Christmas Eve and milk and a piece of cake left for Santa. Delmi recalls presents of a Meccano set, teddy, cricket set ('home made by my father'), Snakes and Ladders, Ludo and Tiddlywinks – these were wrapped in brown paper. Delmi did not attend church or chapel on Christmas Day and recalls Christmas cake, dates and plum puddings to eat.

On Christmas Day there would be a 'fire in the parlour' and the day is remembered with affection. Delmi's worst memory is of 'the whole family having 'flu except for one sister and she ate all the goose over three days!' Delmi never went carol singing but did go out on New Year's Day locally, 'singing and being given money until midday'.

At Easter there were 'new trousers and jersey' and chocolate eggs, but no Easter cards.

For Hallowe'en eyes, nose and mouth were cut out of a swede and a candle put inside.

There were fireworks for November 5th. There would be a large bonfire on the local playing field with a guy and some fireworks – bangers, sparklers and Catherine wheels. The fireworks were bought from a local shop who allowed you only five.

Jean Gardner (née Howells)
(Brought up at The Valley, Llanteg – born 23 November 1941)

'Looking over the questions brought back so many memories of my childhood and how I spend my time with my family over the Christmas period.

For us at The Valley it was a very busy period starting at the beginning of December. There were five of us at the farm – my mother, grandfather, grandmother, and myself, along with my cousin Patrick Watts who always lived with us, and was brought up as my brother and one of the family.

My earliest memories of the Christmas celebrations started first in Ludchurch Infant School with Miss Jones reading a story of Mary, Joseph and the birth of Jesus - I was always fascinated by the story.

In school the making of Chinese paper lanterns signalled the start of Advent. All the pupils would take part in making them, then they would be hung from the ceiling – everyone would take part in cutting out different shaped flags to make coloured bunting to decorate the classrooms. In the infant class, we would draw Christmas trees, crescent moons and star shapes on coloured paper; and then cut out the shapes to hang from the ceiling beams. The older children would cut out from the paper the shapes of capital letters, which, when put together, spelt out 'A MERRY CHRISTMAS' and the bunting was then strung across the front of the class. Each of the classes would make paper chain trimmings with small strips of coloured paper which we stuck together with a glue paste. Other decorations would be made from sheets of coloured crepe paper; the paper would be cut into thin strips and then paired with different coloured pieces and plaited together – other lengths of coloured strips would be mixed and twisted in a barley twirl and strung across the ceilings.

On the last day of school before the Christmas break assembly would start with morning prayers and a short speech by the headmaster, which was then followed with the singing of carols. The morning class would be a casual and informal affair. The big event of the day was the Christmas lunch where we were all given paper hats to wear; these were made by the older children. Lunch was always special with chicken or pork with sausages and stuffing and lots of vegetables. This was followed with trifle and plum pudding, which we were told had silver joeys (a silver threepenny bit) hidden inside, so we were very careful eating the pudding. I never found a coin or knew of anyone else that found one, but it was always fun searching. After lunch, there was a range of games to be played organized by Mr Rodgers the headmaster and Miss Jones. The games varied from Musical Chairs, Pass the Parcel, Blind-Man's-Bluff and a host of other party activities before we were sent home - exhausted, happy and grateful for the Christmas break.

Home at The Valley farm it really was a busy time of year. Patrick and I had to cut down and collect holly sprigs from the hedgerows that fenced the fields for my grandmother to make holly wreaths to sell at Tenby Market, so it was important that we tried to harvest holly with the berries still on. We also collected mistletoe from the garden of the old ruins, down in the bottom field. In the overgrown garden there were a few big old oak trees where we knew the mistletoe grew. Patrick, who was older than me, had to climb up the trees to cut it down. One particular old tree was quite tall, and the mistletoe high up; but Patrick would climb to the top even when the branches were swaying in the wind. I waited at the bottom of the trees collecting it all as it fell, and fastened the mistletoe into manageable bunches to carry home. Patrick had to be careful not to cut off too much of the mistletoe or he would have a telling-off (granny insisted we leave some of it there growing, not only to feed the wild birds, but also to have a healthy supply for the following year).

One of the messier jobs we had to do was to make culm balls for burning on the kitchen fire. The balls were made from small coal mixed with wet clay that we carried up from the bottom field. In a corner of the yard we would mix first with a shovel an equal amount of coal-dust and wet clay; and then in our wellington boots we would tread it together like someone treading grapes – adding water if the mixture appeared dry – then we would shape it into egg-size balls and lay them out to dry.

Most of the timber on the farm felled by the last season's storms would have been cut into logs and stored in the wood-shed for firewood for the coming winter; but to ensure that we had a plentiful supply of firewood and logs we would have to stack a huge pile near the door for easy use.

Extra water would have to be drawn from the well and brought up from the Well Field for washing, drinking and cooking. All the water had to be carried by hand, Patrick and I would carry one or two buckets at a time; every time one of us went down to the Well Field we would have to carry back a pail of fresh water for the farm – in those days we still did not have piped water on tap.

Because money was very tight during the war years, my mother would have to take on extra work feathering and preparing chickens for Christmas at Llanteglos farm. With my father away from home, serving in the 8th Army in North Africa, along with my grandfather's age and failing health it meant that Patrick and I had to take on extra chores about the farm that my mother and father would normally have been doing. Patrick would have to carry out a lot of the lifting and heavier work about the farm – and at that time he was still not yet into his teens. From the kitchen garden, Patrick would cut sprouts, cabbage, and pull up parsnips, swedes and gather in any other green vegetables; I would stack them in the wheel-barrow and wheel them down to the kitchen for granny and mam to wash ready for market. In the week leading up to

Christmas gramps would kill the ducks and geese that had been pre-ordered and raised specially for the Christmas sale. Granny and mam would feather, clean and dress the birds, and any other poultry or chickens about the farm that were old or had stopped laying would also be killed and sent with granny to sell in Tenby. All rabbits caught on the farm in the week leading up to market day would be gutted and strung in pairs; granny would expect at least a dozen pairs to be caught before Christmas Day. Grandmother's chutneys, piccalillis and preserves were all brought out of dry storage, and the best were sorted out, the jars cleaned and dusted, and prepared along with jars of grandfather's honey to sell in Tenby on the last Saturday before Christmas. It was hard work but everyone helped.

After the Saturday market everyone could relax a little, but the hard work still went on, cows still had to be milked, barns, stables and sheds cleaned out, animals fed and bedded down. On the Sunday, it was our day of rest; but only after the animals had been seen to. For me, it was dressing in my best clothes and getting ready for the morning service in chapel. After breakfast, granny would comb and brush my hair, with her long comb, pulling and tugging at my hair until satisfied that my hair was knot free and my tight curls puffed up naturally. From her chest of drawers, she would bring out my best red dress, my long socks, a clean handkerchief and my best hat. While gramps cleaned and polished my boots, granny would check that my dress had no stains or marks before helping me dress. Before I set off, granny would hand me my wicker basket with a slab of fresh butter and loaf of bread to drop off at Aunty Becky on the way – with instructions to bring home the Sunday newspaper for gramps. After one final inspection, granny would press a threepenny bit in my hand for the chapel collection before seeing me off across the road. After lunch it was retracing my steps with mam back to the chapel for the afternoon Sunday School – and to take part in the nativity play with some of the other children. After the play, there was a carol service where everyone joined in, followed by tea and biscuits for the adults, the children were all treated to a glass of home-made lemonade – before being sent home.

Granny wouldn't come to the service, she would stay at home looking after gramps; but she would keep busy in the afternoon baking bread, and making last minute mince pies, trifles etc. Most of the Christmas fare – Christmas cake and pudding, would already have been made weeks earlier.

On Christmas Eve we would decorate the kitchen-dining room with home-made trimmings made from coloured crepe paper. In the corner by the window gramps would put a small holly tree which he had cut earlier; we would decorate the branches with stars and fancy shapes cut out of cardboard and painted with bright colours. On top of the tree we always had a big silver star that would shine brightly when we lit the oil lamp. On a ceiling beam just inside the door mother would hang a sprig of mistletoe to catch out any unwary visitor. After being caught under it once or twice, Patrick and I always gave the door a wide berth, but it was hilarious when friends, neighbours or relatives got caught underneath, especially if it was one of our cousins.

In the evening gramps listened to the six o'clock news on the wireless. The wireless was battery powered and used sparingly, mostly only to listen to the news and important announcements - Patrick and I would only be allowed to listen to Children's Hour once a week. Electricity would not reach The Valley Farm until 1957. We would sit round the open fire in the kitchen to make toast. Gramps would have banked the fire up with wood logs, and then filled in all the gaps with culm balls. With the poker he would rattle and rake out the ash with great gusto; the noise from the rattling would prompt granny to scold gramps, "George! That noise is enough to wake the dead". Granny would have already cut a few slices of her bread for the toast, and the smell from the fresh cut bread would sharpen the poorest of appetites. With long toasting forks we would toast the bread in front of the glowing embers. Once the bread was toasted on both sides, we would eat it with granny's home-made butter and jam. After cleaning up after supper, mam would bring out her sewing box and, sitting quietly by the table with gran, they would sort through our day clothes, and any that they found that needed repairing she and granny would sew, darn and patch all the rips and tears by the light of the oil lamp. Later gramps would read a few verses out of the Bible, then he and granny would look into the fire and take it in turns to tell us a story. We would then all sing a few hymns and carols before hanging up our socks over the fire before going to bed.

On Christmas morning, I would be so excited – granny, gramps and mam would already be up. Granny and mam would be in the kitchen cooking breakfast and preparing the vegetables for lunch. We always had a goose for Christmas dinner and granny would have already had it in the oven cooking. When Patrick and I dressed and came downstairs, we would have to go straight out to the yard and help gramps with the milking and feeding of the animals, before turning them out in the fields. I would have to go to the henhouse and feed the chickens and collect the eggs while Patrick mucked out in the cowshed with gramps. We were not allowed to go back to the house until all the essential chores were finished. Gramps would light his pipe, and then he would walk slowly round the yard checking on the jobs. Gramps would double check the sheds to ensure that all the oil-lamps had been put out properly and the daily chores completed. Only then when he seemed satisfied that every thing was done that could be done, would he say with a sly grin and a sparkle in his eyes, "Hey maid, you best get back inside the house and see if we had any visitors".

As children, there was never the fuss and expectation with Christmas as we have today. Those of us who were lucky enough to have been given more than one toy as presents, were very few indeed. With a lot of the young men away in the armed services, young boys would be given lead soldiers, toy tanks and military vehicles; others would receive model fighter and bomber airplanes and some, whose fathers were in the navy, got toy warships. Young girls would, if they were lucky, have small dolls and nurses' uniforms. The older children were given books to read or maybe a jigsaw to make quietly in the evenings. The sort of gifts that our generation would have received were more in the way of warm clothing - woollen gloves, mittens and socks, for which we were very grateful. Girls would have been given hats, scarves or handkerchiefs, boys would get mittens, balaclavas or long socks; most of these would have been hand-knitted at home during the long autumn evenings.

Christmas was special, not only because of the religious significance, but also because it gave families, friends and the community a chance to gather and celebrate together. Those people in the community who had husbands, wives, sons and daughters away on war duties, found it gave them much needed support. Their absent loved ones, if they could, would somehow manage to find a day off over Christmas to get home; even if it was only for just a few hours. There would be a knock on the door, and then pandemonium, but the visits always seemed short and hurried, with never enough time to swap news and gossip, and in what seemed only a few moments in time, the visitor was off to see another of his or her relatives, leaving the house, for a few moments, quietly sombre.

Back in the house on Christmas morning, it was with great excitement and anticipation that Patrick and I looked for the socks we hung in front of the fire the night before. I remember one particular Christmas finding my sock not hung up on the line where I left it, but on the floor by the side of the brass fender. Alongside my sock was a much larger parcel; it was far too big to fit into the sock – I remember granny saying I was a very lucky girl to have been left an extra present. I decided to keep that particular gift until the very last before opening. I always took great care in opening the presents that were in my sock. I would take out one of the small parcels, and examine it minutely, then slowly I would unwrap the gift - trying not to rip the paper. Our presents were always wrapped in brown paper and tied with parcel string – the paper and string was as much the present as the wrapped contents, as the paper could be used later for drawing or writing on. Even if I didn't use it, mam or gran would find some use for it.

The first present that I opened was a small book of the New Testament, a gift from my father. The cover was bound and intricately carved in olive wood that had been grown in Palestine; at the time that was where my father was stationed. Laying the book aside for further examination later, I knew what the book was, but it was not something exciting that I could eat or play with. I was soon back delving into my sock looking for my next parcel; then I unpacked strips of coloured modelling clay (plasticine). Later in the day, that particular gift would keep me and gramps entertained and fill almost our entire evening making models of the farm and the animals that lived on it. Then I unpacked a parcel containing a box of crayons and a colouring book, also there was a small bar of chocolate that I found in amongst the nuts – which was a real treat. Then I came across a small bag of sweets, a mixture of mints and granny's homemade toffee (very hard and chewy, but delicious; you would pop a piece in your mouth, and you would still be chewing on it an hour later). Chocolate and sweets were still on ration, and we were only allowed two ounces a week. In the war years, chocolates and sweets were something that we never had often, only on very special occasions. The smell of the ripe apples wafting up from the sock as I uncovered the fruit was delicious. Amongst the small parcels were piles of nuts, they were mostly hazelnuts, but there were some walnuts; granny would have got these and the oranges from Mr Handicott, the greengrocer in Tenby. The hazelnuts were the ones we had picked and gathered ourselves during the past autumn months. Granny would have bagged the nuts in old flour sacks and stored them away up in the rafters until now – it was still a wonderful thrill, and a treat finding the nuts after so long, mixed amongst the different packages in our socks. Right at the bottom of the sock, swelling and plumping out the toe space, was always a large orange; it was always a struggle to retrieve it.

I had been too engrossed in discovering what presents were in my sock to have been watching much of what treasures Patrick was unpacking from his. The fruit, nuts, sweets and chocolate that Patrick found in his sock would have been much the same as mine. The value of the contents would have been almost identical, except that he, being a boy, and older than me, his presents were much more grown-up than what I received. I remember him unpacking from his sock a set of colouring pencils, a wooden ruler and pencil box, drawing and painting books; there was a small box of water paints, and he also had a jigsaw, which I helped him make in the evenings. Alongside his sock he found two parcels, both parcels contained books; I remember a boy's adventure book and a *Rupert the Bear* book. He also had a small hand-held game where we would take it turns to shoot a metal ball around a board to score, in a game of pot the ball.

It was time for me to open my biggest parcel. I had no idea what to expect – but I could feel my mother, granny and gramps all watching as I revealed a beautiful rag doll with long black hair. The hair was made from braided yarn; the long strands were woven intricately down over the side of her head ending in two plaits that were tied at the end with silk red bows. For her eyes, she had two black mother-of-pearl buttons. She was dressed in a deep red velvety dress with black ankle-length socks. I fell in love with her straight away and named her Sally. It was the first doll that I ever received and I was ever so pleased with the gift. Even though I treasured her, I had little time to play with her; I never took her outdoors to play with, in case I got her dirty - she was always kept by the fire in a corner on gramp's chair. It was only in the evenings after all the chores were finished, that I had time to sit and play with my favourite present, Sally, my rag doll.'

Doreen Glanville
(Brought up in Pembroke Dock – with Llanteg connections –
born 29 November 1939)

Only once does Doreen recall having a fir Christmas tree. Decorations were home-made paper chains and she does not remember any holly or ivy. The family sent Christmas cards, which depicted religious scenes or robins.

Hugh and Doreen Glanville

Doreen put up a stocking which would then contain an orange, apple and nuts – she would also get a main present, such as crayons and a colouring book. These would be opened Christmas morning. 'I remember a doll's house and my mother making the furniture'.

The family ate chicken for Christmas dinner, with all the trimmings – but no crackers. They also went to church.

Doreen's best memory of Christmas is 'waking on Christmas morning to see what presents I had, and then visiting all our relatives to see what they had, too'.

For New Year's Eve Doreen went round to all their family who lived nearly, and it was customary for the first visitor of the New Year to be a dark-haired man.

At Easter there were no chocolate eggs but 'after painting a hard-boiled egg we went egg trundling and rolled them down the hill'. There would always be some new clothing at Easter - 'maybe a bonnet' - and cards were also recalled.

For November 5th a few fireworks and sparklers were set off in the street but there was no bonfire.

Lyn Harcombe
(Brought up at Tonypandy - with Llanteg connections –
born 16 March 1937)

'Christmas would never seem to arrive. The waiting from about November onwards seemed interminable. The excitement on Christmas Eve was beyond description.

It would all start with my mother making the Christmas cake and pudding. The pudding was boiled in a muslin cloth for hours on end and the smell was wonderful. Sometimes we had a small pudding after Sunday dinner just to make sure it was all right. Then came the icing of the cake and out would come the decorations from previous years – the Father Christmas, small fir trees, the sleigh and reindeer; all carefully cleaned and wrapped in paper from one year to the next.

The house was always decorated with home-made trimmings – endless paper chains, lanterns, a 'real' Christmas tree, a twig of mistletoe (if we were lucky enough to find some in the shop) and holly picked from local bushes. The tree was decorated with tinsel and fairy lights (which had been carefully checked by my father and then equally carefully packed away the previous year). There would always be a fairy on top of the tree.

We always seemed to have Christmas cards so I suppose we must have sent some as well.

My mother would cook her own mince pies and we always made sure that there were some left for Santa – I think poor Rudolph had to make do with a carrot!

Christmas presents were very few and far between. We always had a stocking at the bottom of the bed and it was always filled by Santa – nuts of different types in the toe, an orange or a tangerine, an apple, chocolates and the "main present" at the top. Sometimes we would have a board game between the four children.

Then there was Christmas dinner. The turkey was always too large to be cooked in our own oven so we would have to take it to the bakery in the next street to have it cooked. My mother would make the stuffing with a little help from us children. The meal was a special event – we would have serviettes, umpteen knives, forks and spoons and the table would be laid with the "special" tablecloth. My father always said grace before eating this meal, something he never usually did. The meal was always too large and we ate too much but we always had room for a little piece of pudding with white sauce – but no brandy. I could never understand how each one of us managed to get a threepenny piece in our pudding – and never more than one each!

After dinner we would all sit and listen to the Queen on the radio. Then it was time for games – Ludo, Monopoly, card games, Snakes and Ladders, quizzes etc., and to indulge in our chocolates and sweets. By night time we were very tired - too full to eat much tea and ready for bed.

Boxing Day was a bit of an anticlimax and we did very little – cold turkey for dinner and turkey in various forms for the rest of the week. I can't remember when we ate the pork and the gammon!

We always went to chapel three times on Sunday but we never went on Christmas Day; we all assumed it was because there were so many other things to do, and anyway, my mother was busy cooking the Christmas dinner. The radio was always on on Christmas morning and we enjoyed all the carol singing even though we never went ourselves.

New Year was a non-event during my childhood. We always went to bed at the usual time of about 7 o'clock. I have no idea whether my parents stayed up to celebrate the event. I remember my brother going out on New Year's Day to be the first to greet people since he had a mop of curly hair and that was supposedly lucky.

My only memory of Easter was the Sunday School Parade. We all had to march through Tonypandy dressed in "Sunday best" and the ladies (and girls) all had new clothes. I hated the whole exercise!

Hallowe'en was ducking-apple night when we all got very wet. Sometimes the apples were hung from the ceiling by string – this was the only treat of the day.

I'm afraid I have no memories at all of bonfire night – apart from making a guy with old clothes stuffed with straw and paper. I suppose we must have burnt the guy somewhere but I have no idea where – strange how this night is a blank!'

Josephine Jenkins
(Brought up at Velfrey Road, Whitland - with Llanteg connections - born on 21 May 1938)

There was no tree at Christmas but Josephine recalls twisted crepe paper decorations and home-made chains. They also used holly and mistletoe (the smallest piece).

No Christmas cards are remembered – 'probably because of expense'.

As far as presents went, Josephine could never recall not having anything – presents were usually only books. 'Even today the smell of a new book is lovely. We saw them Christmas morning and they weren't wrapped. Also there were games like Ludo and Draughts. My first book at home, or the first one that I remember, was *Three Little Kittens Have Lost Their Mittens,* and there were always Rupert Annuals – the books from the Church were always reading books.' Josephine put up a stocking – and received a few sweets and a little fruit. A mince pie was left out for Santa.

The food Josephine mostly recalls eating at Christmas is 'sweets, probably not many'.

Josephine's best memory is - 'I suppose the excitement of it all. The lovely smells of the extra cooking, and the unusual smells of fruit. I remember back to war time, and I suppose there was a shortage of everything'.

There are no bad memories, 'but I was probably aware that what we were given were rare treats.

I suppose the Church Christmas Party was a highlight – there were small gifts, usually fruit, and I think it was there that we were presented with books for faithful attendance at Sunday School.

We used to go around singing on New Year's Day morning, usually around Velfrey Road.'

No Easter eggs or cards are recalled.

For November 5th there would be a bonfire and fireworks; someone made a guy (usually a group of boys). Most fireworks were set off in the Quoit Field (the playing field at the bottom of the road) – 'it was a communal thing'.

Nancy John (née Phillips)

(Brought up at The Folly, Llanteg – born 13 September 1931)
Nancy recalls putting up coloured paper chains and bells for Christmas. There would also be 'lots of holly' – but no tree is remembered. The decorating would be done before Christmas Eve. Some decorations were home-made while others were bought. Christmas cards were also sent, mostly showing Father Christmas, snowmen and various nativity scenes.

Nancy 'really believed' in Santa until she was about ten years old.

She recalls waiting for him to arrive, and also balloons being on her bed. A carrot would be left out for the reindeer and a pillow case put out for the presents.

Presents would be opened Christmas morning and Nancy recalls 'lovely presents – dolls, books and I remember a tea set - relatives were good to me. Mrs Jackett, my Godmother, sent me a threepenny bit'. Nancy's favourite books were *Sunny Stories* (Enid Blyton) and *Rupert Bear*.

A special Christmas cake would be made by Nancy's mother and the family had chicken for Christmas dinner. There would also be Christmas pudding and sometimes crackers.

The family would go to church and chapel but Nancy does not recall whether they went on Christmas Day. Nancy's best memories are of 'singing and reciting in the concerts – we loved Christmas'.

Nancy's worst memory is of 'when someone broke my doll on Christmas Day morning!'

She would also go carol singing – usually around the closer houses of Oaklands, Belview, Sandy Grove, Middleton and Blackheath.

On New Year's Eve Nancy always went to visit at York House and sang with her cousin Sylvia at Summerbrook (Mr and Mrs Mortimer), Llanteglos and Heatherland.

On New Year's Day Nancy visited her Aunt Polly and Uncle Alby (father's brother) at The Factory, Amroth, and slept the night. Nancy believes it was customary to stay there every New Year (her uncle worked at Amroth Castle).

For Easter there would be chocolate eggs as presents, some from Nancy's mother's sister in Kent. Her uncle was lighthouse keeper at Strumble Head and 'we went to stay twice a year at Goodwick and went to the lighthouse for tea'.

There were new clothes for Easter - 'we always went to Carmarthen for a new outfit, bought at Kings in Carmarthen. We went by bus and each time I felt awful as I was a poor traveller. We always had fish and chips in the same cafe. Mum took me to see Shirley Temple films in Tenby'.

Photo: Nancy John

*L: Nancy John (née Phillips) with her mother Fanny (seated centre)
on the latter's 100th Birthday - 7 June 1999*

Violet Merriman (née Thomas and sister to Peter Thomas – see below)
(Brought up in Kilgetty - with Llanteg connections – born 5 December 1932)
Violet recalls home-made paper chains and a Christmas tree which was a holly bush - 'we put Vaseline on the leaves and stuck on cotton wool to look like snow'.

189

Decorations were put up on Christmas Eve along with holly. Violet does not remember Christmas cards. Father Christmas is recalled as an old man with white beard and dressed in red who 'would call if you had been very good'. Presents were opened Christmas morning after church – there would be an apple, orange, nuts, hankie, book (*Sunny Stories*) and maybe a ribbon. A stocking was hung up and the presents would not be wrapped.

There would be chicken for Christmas dinner with sprouts and pudding and Christmas cake, plus mince pies and jaffa oranges.

Violet's best memories are of 'a very warm and friendly atmosphere, playing games and singing carols'. Her worst memory is 'of my dad being away during the war'.

Violet also went carol singing around Kilgetty.

For New Year's Eve Violet would go 'to a lady just over the road from us – and my brother would go outside just before midnight and then come back in after midnight carrying a parcel with a piece of coal and a sixpence and something else I can't remember. One year mam decided that we'd do the same and when we got home after midnight the little parcel had been taken off the doorstep; someone had a shock when they opened it!'

Violet recalls her first Easter egg when she was about seven. It was given to her by 'a young lad in the village – it was quite large, had no paper around it –just a red ribbon, and it was empty'. There would also always be 'a new suit of clothes for church'.

There would be a bonfire for November 5th, no fireworks are remembered but they did have 'baked potatoes and sausages in the fire'.

Beryl Payne

(Brought up in Cardiff - with Llanteg connections – born 4 May 1923) At Christmas the house would be decorated with paper chains, tinsel and Christmas cards. The family had a fir Christmas tree, which was put up a few days before Christmas. The decorations were partly home-made – 'often made in school'. There was also holly and mistletoe, with the mistletoe being bought at a local store. Christmas cards were sent, showing 'old-time scenes and a ho-ho Father Christmas on his sleigh'.

A stocking was hung up on Christmas Eve, with mince pies being left for Santa. Presents were wrapped in coloured paper and Beryl can recall 'games, books and various "surprises"'.

On Christmas morning the family attended church for the 7am service (Beryl recalls having to get up at 6.30am!) Later there would be crackers, with chicken for dinner, and plum pudding.

Some of Beryl's best Christmas memories are of 'wonderful family gatherings on Christmas Day, Boxing Day and New Year's Eve'; and she says she has 'wonderful memories of childhood Christmases in Cardiff'. Again there are no bad Christmas memories.

Beryl went carol singing to local neighbours.

New Year's Eve would be spent with neighbours, and it was customary to stay up until midnight.

At Easter there would be chocolate eggs and sometimes new clothes. No special games are recalled but Beryl says 'we had a great time and I have lots of happy memories now!'

Nothing was done for Hallowe'en but there were fireworks with neighbours on November 5th, sometimes a guy. The fireworks were bought from local shops and the bonfire was in the garden.

Kathleen Phillips (née Mathias)
(Brought up at Little Ludchurch, Pendeilo and Parcsaison – born 29 January 1929)

Kathleen recalls that the family sent Christmas cards – 'with robins, coaching views, and religious themes'. They usually had a Christmas tree and decorated the house with garlands, holly and ivy. Presents were opened on Christmas Day and Kathleen remembers 'a lovely red dress. I still have some of the toys I was given – especially a rather dishevelled teddy bear over 70 years old!'

A stocking was put up and presents were always wrapped decoratively.

For Christmas dinner the family would have chicken and sometimes turkey, with sprouts, tangerines and plum pudding. There were crackers, and it was tradition for families to go to church on Christmas Eve.

'As my mother was a very good cook and we lived on a farm, we never went short of food and mother was ingenious enough to conjure up Christmas presents despite the shortages of wartime rationing.' Kathleen has no bad memories of Christmas but wonders 'were Christmases colder then, or was it just that few houses had central heating?'

'I remember one year when a large group of us from Ludchurch walked across fields visiting houses carol singing. For light we carried

191

lanterns on poles.' They would go all around the village.

'I always visited my grandfather and aunt on Christmas Day. My grandfather gave me a bicycle during the war years when they were in very short supply. It was totally black – not a vestige of chrome in sight, but it was a pleasure to ride. And can anyone remember a back-pedaller (press the pedal backwards and it acted like a brake)?'

For Easter it was the fashion to have new clothes to be worn when attending chapel or church.

Regarding November 5th, Kathleen recalls – 'I remember my father rather foolishly set off a "jackie jumper" firework in the house once and it travelled from one room to another – great consternation was caused!'

James Smart
(Brought up in Compton Bassett and born on 26 August 1935 – now living at West Llanteg)

James recalls that decorations were put up before Christmas Eve – they had a fir tree, home-made paper chains and some 'rather nice shop ones'. They also used holly, ivy and mistletoe which was gathered from his grandfather's estate. Christmas cards were sent with hunting, inns, churches and village scenes.

Presents were opened on Christmas morning and were some toys but 'mostly books', and James would put up a stocking – 'and sometimes a pillow case'. Presents were always wrapped – sometimes with coloured paper, sometimes brown. Santa was lucky and would be left mince pies and some home-made wine.

For Christmas dinner the family would have goose with all the trimmings, and crackers.

If the family were joining the grandparents they always attended church on Christmas Day.

James's best memories of Christmas are of 'carol singers, snow, skating, family parties, my grandfather always leading the singing'.

Not so pleasant are recollections of 'cold old houses, wearing lots of jumpers' – but there were also 'warm kitchens' to make up for it.

There would be a big Christmas Party at the village hall - when he was six James helped cut the Christmas cake there – and of course there would be a Father Christmas attending. There would also be big parties at his grandparents and they visited other houses in the village by pony and trap.

At Easter there was 'hunt the egg in my grandparents' garden'.

For bonfire night there would be a 'large fire in my grandparents' field', with fireworks supplied by them and potatoes and punch for refreshments.

Laura Thomas (née Davies)
(Brought up at Greenacre and Stanwell, Llanteg)

Laura recalls decorating with holly and ivy, and of mostly having a Christmas tree which would have been a holly bush. The decorating was done on Christmas Eve. Newspaper would also be cut into strips and made into a chain – these would not have been coloured or painted.

The family would send Christmas cards – 'to relatives in America and friends and relatives living a distance away'. The cards were bought at Mrs Raymond's shop at The Laurels and were decorated with Christmas scenes and snowmen.

Father Christmas was believed in until 'my brother Bob found the toys on the top of the wardrobe!' Santa was imagined to be as he was depicted on Christmas cards.

The presents in the stocking consisted of 'an orange, an apple and some monkey nuts. Bob had a van one Christmas and we all shared it'. Gifts were opened at 6am before going to church. A stocking was always put up but 'no presents were wrapped' and no food was left out for Santa.

For Christmas lunch there would be beef or a chicken, also sprouts, dates and oranges. There would be mince pies and Christmas cake and puddings – 'we used to boil four together in the boiler'.

Laura attended Amroth Church with her mother for the 6am service.

Best memories of Christmas are 'of going round all the neighbours carol singing for pennies with a group of school friends, having a school party and concert, also the Sunday School party. We used to take a pudding down to an elderly neighbour, Mrs Scourfield, who lived at Stanwell (we lived at Greenacre until I was nine years old)'. There are no bad memories of Christmas. The carol singing was done 'around Llanteg and back – down the Lower Road and back along the Upper Road (*A477*) meeting friends as we went'.

Laura recalls singing in the choir at Crunwere Church - Howard James from Blackheath used to play the pedal organ for tonic solfa. 'We (all the local children) used to go up to the Mountain Field to slide – we all had hob-nails in our boots.

We used to have two concerts a year at Crunwere School for the church – everyone used to take part – all the generations. One was before Christmas and one would be about February.

On New Year's Eve we went to Church Evensong. New Year's Day we would kill the pigs and we went round the neighbours with some 'fry' (they returned the gift when they killed their pigs).'

Laura did not stay up till midnight on New Year's Eve or send Easter cards but 'we used to like to have a new hat for Easter, and my mother would send off to Oxendales' catalogue for this treat. Easter was very religious. From Palm Sunday through Holy Week we were not allowed to do any activity which gave enjoyment. The whole week was treated like a Sunday – we were not allowed to play.

At Hallowe'en the family tradition was that my father used to hang an apple and a candle from the hooks in the ceiling. We used to bite the apple – whichever of us bit the apple would have the prize of a sweet. On November 5th we used to go up to The Mountain and burn the gorse.'

Peter Thomas
(Brought up in Kilgetty - with Llanteg connections –
born 7 June 1937)

Peter recalls a Christmas tree and 'mainly home-made decorations, like paper chains, made from scraps of used packing paper, all colours and cut into strips to make chains, also cardboard cut-outs of santas and snowmen which were coloured in with crayons'. The Christmas tree would be a holly bush 'with Vaseline smeared onto the leaves to stick some cotton wool to give a snow effect'.

The family sent Christmas cards – 'mainly to neighbours. These were home-made of thin cardboard or stiff white paper, using greaseproof paper to copy the designs (Father Christmas, snowmen and Christmas trees)'.

A glass of milk would be left out for Santa, and Peter would hang one of his socks at the end of the bed. Presents would usually be wrapped in brown paper. Inside the sock Peter would find 'a handful of mixed nuts, an apple, an orange and (if lucky) a handful of sweets which was eaten during the day'.

There were no crackers but 'we always had turkey or chicken with the usual trimmings of potatoes, cabbage and swedes, also home-made mince pies, cake and pudding'.

Peter's best memories are of 'Christmas Day and of carol singing around every house in Kilgetty – but then the village was not as big as it is now'. There are no bad Christmas memories.

For November 5th there would be a bonfire at the bottom of the garden with the family and a 'few older neighbours gathered around – we always made a guy, which was made from old clothes from the neighbours. We always bought our fireworks in Pembroke Fair on a travelling stand; they were called "wallops" and they had a heck of a big bang'.

The late George Vincent
(Brought up in Port Talbot - with Llanteg connections –
born 20 May 1917)

Mr Vincent can recall crepe paper streamers and holly in the house at Christmas. There was no Christmas tree, all the decorations were home-made and the mistletoe was bought from the local market. The family did send cards, which were 'mostly of a religious nature'. Father Christmas was a 'portly figure with a long white beard, dressed in a red cloak'. A stocking would be left out on Christmas Eve and some presents remembered are a 'football, magic lantern, hoop and skip', which would have been opened on Christmas morning (having been wrapped in coloured paper).

The family always went to chapel on Christmas Day, with mince pies, Christmas cake and plum pudding (with threepenny pieces) for later.

Mr Vincent went out carol singing 'to neighbours'. His best memories of Christmas are of 'the food being plentiful and of new bedding for doll's cot' – he has no bad memories of Christmas. For New Year's Eve the family visited neighbours.

At Easter Mr Vincent received chocolate eggs, but there were no Easter cards. There would also be new clothes - 'trousers or a jumper'.

Nothing special was done for Hallowe'en but Mr Vincent did bob apples. There were no celebrations for November 5th.

APPENDIX

LLANTEG HISTORY SOCIETY MEMBERS

After a suggestion a few years ago we thought we would belatedly introduce ourselves to you.

Our group has remained pretty much with the same membership since its beginnings in 1999 – apart from deaths and people leaving the district. However to compensate we have gained some new members who have moved into the village.

Chairman

Tony Brinsden has been involved with the group since its inception and Chairman for most of that time. Tony's ancestors can be traced back in the area for over 250 years.

196

Secretary

Ruth Roberts has been Secretary since 1999 and her family tree joins into Tony's a few generations back.

Treasurer

John Lewis-Tunster has also been with the group since 1999 and Treasurer since 2005 when Judith Lloyd moved away. John can also trace his roots in the area back over 250 years and his family tree joins into that of Ruth and Tony above.

Past Treasurer

Judith Lloyd, who, although now living in Leicestershire, has to be included here as from 1999-2005 she was a great support in all our ventures and is still Editor of all our books and booklets.

Members

Margaret Brinsden – originally from Whitland – now living in Llanteg and is married to our Chairman.

Alan Davies – has connections with the village through his ancestors.

Eirwen Davies – has lived in the village for over 50 years and resides in what is probably the oldest property in the parish, Trenewydd, which dates back to at least 1568.

Maureen Ebsworth – was born and brought up at Upper Marros Farm and knows many of the older Llanteg families through farming connections. Has always been interested in local history and joined the group in 2002.

Audrey James – originally from Whitland but has lived here for over 50 years and married into an old Llanteg family, the Jameses of Bevlin.

Mollie James – married to Hugh James who is now 92 years old and can also trace his family tree back over 250 years, his ancestors joining into those of Tony, John and Ruth (above).

Dilys Jenkinson – a new member since 2008. Dilys lives just outside the village at Lower Pendeilo.

Jane Lawrence – from a well known local family whose ancestors also join into those of Ruth (above).

Katherine Lloyd – from Carmarthen but her ancestors once lived in the village at The Laurels.

Caroline Mason – whose family has long connections with village and whose husband's line links in to that of Tony, Ruth and John above.

Winifred Tunster – mother of John (above) and also has long family connections with the village.

Owen Vaughan with wife Carol

Owen J.Vaughan – joined the society in 2002. Researched Llanteg village happenings and the Oriels of Llanteg 1725–1973 and the surname origin back to Spittal in 1482.

Ruth Webb   *Andy Webb*

Ruth and Andy Webb – moved to the village in 2003 and are now very active members of the group.

Past Members

Nikki Banner
Kathleen and Eric Davies
Brenda and Alan Stevens

In Remembrance

Bob Davies – an uncle of Tony Brinsden (above).

Wyn Lawrence – husband of Jane Lawrence (above).

Desmond Wolff – son of one time Headmaster of Crunwere School, Mr F.E.C.Wolff.

Even though most of us appear to have long connections with the village and surrounding area it is by no means compulsory! We were all very much beginners when the group was formed and we always appreciate new members – whether they are local or not. In fact it was Judith's enthusiasm that helped us get our books published and she had moved here from England and had no village connections - also Ruth and Andy Webb are also very active members. So everyone is most welcome as we all have something to contribute.

Bibliography

Pembrokeshire County History Volume VIII (Pembrokeshire Record Office)

Crunwere Wills and Inventories

Returns for Crunwere Jury Service (Pembrokeshire Record Office)

Pembrokeshire Parliamentary Election Poll Book (Pembrokeshire Record Office)

Narberth Union Abstract and History of Paupers 1872-1882 (Pembrokeshire Record Office)

Trade Directories (Carmarthen Record Office)

Register of Inquests Held (Pembrokeshire Record Office)

Papers of Lewis and James Solicitors, Narberth (Pembrokeshire Record Office)

Dalton Genealogical Society papers

St Peter's Church website

Land Tax Assessment Papers (Pembrokeshire Record Office)

Y Brycheiniog

Cymmrodorion Society Journal Vol. 13 2007

King Charles the Martyr Society

Pembrokeshire Life Magazine

Parish Censuses (Pembrokeshire Record Office)

Private Papers relating to Mountain Chapel

Mountain Chapel, Building Recording and Graveyard Survey Cambria Archaeology 2003/119

De Rutzen Sales Notice of 1904

Narberth Weekly News – various years

Western Mail 1985

Carmarthen Journal 2006

Funeral Reports – Narberth Weekly News

Charles F.Shepherd's *St Elidyr, Crunwere - A Historical Note* 1933

St Elidyr's Crunwere Minute Book 1941-79

Christmas Custom Questionnaires - Llanteg History Society